Greetings, Harry

Regards from many
years of friendship

Henry

FOOTPRINTS OF THE BAKER BOY

Editor: Gaye LeBaron
Book Designer: Brad Cott
Manuscript Editor: Mary Fricker

First Printing 2014
Copyright ©2014 by H. F. Trione
All Rights Reserved

Printed by Lithocraft II, Santa Rosa, CA
Printed in the United States of America
ISBN # 978-0-615-97007-3

FOOTPRINTS OF THE BAKER BOY

By Henry F. Trione

O wad some Power the giftie gie us
To see oursel's as ithers see us!

~ Robert Burns

From: "To a Louse, On Seeing One on a Lady's Bonnet at Church"

Dedication

To the three important people in my life –
my mother, Catherine;
my wife of 56 years, Madelyne,
and my present wife, Eileen –
for the pleasant life they have given me.

~ ~ ~ ~ ~

And to God's greatest gifts,
my two sons, Victor and Mark.
With their wives, Karen and Cathy,
and their children and grandchildren,
I count them my closest friends.

Acknowledgements

I gratefully acknowledge the assistance and support of editor Gaye LeBaron, my assistant Stacey Garrison, book designer Brad Cott, manuscript editor Mary Fricker and consultant David Nelson. Without their aid, this project would still be a work in progress.

TABLE OF CONTENTS

Foreword

Chapter I ~ The First Generation **15**
Chapter II ~ Teenage Years **22**
Chapter III ~ College Years **29**
Chapter IV ~ Navy Years (1942-1946) **37**
Chapter V ~ Getting on with Business **49**
Chapter VI ~ Sonoma Mortgage **54**
Chapter VII ~ Wells Fargo **65**

Part Two

Chapter VIII ~ Timberrrr! **72**
Chapter IX ~ Win Some, Lose Some **81**
Chapter X ~ Empire College **85**
Chapter XI ~ The Fruit of the Vine **90**
Chapter XII ~ The Oakland Raiders **101**
Chapter XIII ~ How I Got My Ranger Hat **106**
Chapter XIV ~ My Life with Horses **113**
Chapter XV ~ Trifling with Truffles **123**
Chapter XVI ~ Wildlife **132**
Chapter XVII ~ Checking My List **143**

Afterword

Twice Blessed **153**
Pats on the Back **155**
Quotations I've Remembered **158**

FOREWORD

By John Reed, MD

These memoirs reflect a lifetime of reminiscing with friends, telling and polishing stories, sharpening them as only a great raconteur can do. The quality of story telling is very high indeed. Only a man with the most remarkable gift for friendship could have done it.

There are stand-alone chapters that will reach out and grab you. Skip to "The Fruit of the Vine," "The Oakland Raiders," "Trifling with Truffles" or "Wildlife." You won't know whether to read forward or backwards, but you'll be hooked. This book is a terrific read. One of the questions I asked was, "How did you remember all this?" It turned out that he has, over all these years, kept a desk calendar so complete that I was able to learn the exact date I first met Henry – July 2nd, 1974. This remarkable bit of record keeping, as it turns out, is revealing but not directly related to the creation of the memoir.

Like all good memoirs (which reflect the time and the place as well as the personal history), it is a book about more than the memoirist. It's a book about a generation, a book about opportunity, success, and responsibility and, as Henry would insist, luck.What wasn't luck at all, however, was what he made and gave of his success. His personality, generosity, and capacity for both friendship and leadership have been integral to the history and evolution of Sonoma County and Santa Rosa for very nearly 70 years.

Physical endurance is one of Henry's God-given gifts, one that has seen him into his 10th decade. But the more important virtues, amounting to a kind of moral endurance, are attributes that came from his mother and father and the culture that produced them. That is a central fact of his life. Henry's father died before the age of 60. Henry has survived five potentially mortal illnesses. The contrast seems always to have left him with a sense of what might have been. It may be what drives him to demand the most out of every day. There is a certain tone to the generations of families with strong fathers. Through Henry, his father can be seen very clearly, and we can also add that he lived a life to make a father proud.

Never failing to act upon a personal philosophy about sharing good fortune, he has been the magnetic center for the philanthropy of his generation and that generation has been transformational in our history.

This is a wonderful memoir. I am not in the least surprised.

CHAPTER I ~ THE FIRST GENERATION

Both my mother and father came from the very northern part of Italy. The province of Piemonte borders Switzerland to the north and France to the west. My mother was born in Pont-Canavese, a small city known for its production of copper artifacts and many flourishing cotton and woolen mills. My father, one of seven children in a prominent business family, was born in the neighboring small city of Cuorgné. My parents' families had lived in these respective locales for generations. To understand what happened in their lives, you have to understand Italian history. This subject has, for obvious reasons, has been of interest to me.

Italy is composed of 20 different provinces, somewhat similar to our states. Over the centuries, due to limited transportation and communication, each province developed its own dialect to the extent that one was quite different from another. People from the north – Piemonte, Lombardy, Genoa – on down to the southern regions of Calabria and Sicily maintained their own identity, each certain that their region was superior. In 1870, Giuseppe Garibaldi, a general and statesman, united the country into a single monarchy. In this "Risorgimento," as the unification was called, the provinces maintained their separate customs and dialects.

When Benito Mussolini was in power, he decreed that Italy's official language would be the Florentine dialect. His intention was to create language uniformity in the schools and government institutions. But, even today, many Italians are bilingual, still speaking their own provincial dialect as well as the official Florentine. For example, the Piemontese dialect my parents learned from childhood had French roots and nuances from its location near the French border.

In the late 18th century there was a worldwide economic depression that lasted until after World War I. The "hard times" in Europe was a prime factor that motivated substantial immigration to the United States, Argentina, Australia and elsewhere, which continued for several decades. As in most emigration patterns,

~ 15 ~

individuals and families tended to move in the company of those from their province and keep the old-country traditions alive in their new homes. Italians who settled in cities like New York, Boston, San Francisco and Buenos Aires followed tradition.

Interestingly enough, through the years, the children of these immigrant families have married non-Italians, most predominantly the Irish, I think. As a consequence of this co-mingling of ethnicity, many with Italian names are what I jokingly call "half-breeds" while I am proudly announcing myself as a "full-blood." My sons, I like to point out to them, are "half-breeds."

In the early years of the 20th century, a great many Italians from various provinces established themselves in the San Francisco area. North Beach was completely Italian, much as Chinatown was solidly Chinese. My parents were in the midst of this immigration pattern that would prove so significant in the development of Northern California and the Bay Area.

My father, born in 1889, immigrated to the United States in 1905, immediately after completing the European equivalent of high school. The economy in the town where he was born, Cuorgné, was dependent on stone quarries that were the primary source of building materials for the region. My father's family had been in the stone mining business for several generations. He seemed to leave any interest in his home region behind when he came to the United States, and didn't talk about it; but I surmise the family was of middle income and had a business background.

I have visited Cuorgné four times and have seen the Trione home that still stands on Via Trione. It's a three-story building, made of the stone from the quarries, perhaps even the family quarries. Also, in the mountains just north of Cuorgné there is a small crossroad with an area called Trione. On one of my "roots trips" to Cuorgné, I walked through the local cemetery and found a number of Trione headstones, with dates going back several generations. A recent Internet search tallied 167 families named Trione in Italy, with 67 of them in Piemonte. So, despite the wholesale departure of so many at the turn of the 20th century, the family ties to Northern Italy remain strong.

There were many reasons for this migration. One was the strict adherence to the old Roman law of primogeniture, which meant that the oldest son was the inheritor of all the family's land and wealth. My father, being the sixth of seven children, could hold no hope for a share of the family business. Thus, he opted, as did so many like him, to strike out on his own.

I believe, from what little I could learn about his first years in the United States, that Vittorio, my father, went first to Arizona where he intended to join one of his older brothers. He worked in the mines there and then, for reasons I have not been able to trace, he moved to Washington State and, finally, came to be part of the growing Piemontese community in San Francisco.

In 1915, he and a cousin, James Camerlo, purchased the bakery in Fortuna, some 300 miles north of San Francisco, in Humboldt County. I've always been curious but never learned just how the two of them "found" Fortuna. The roads were so bad as to be practically non-existent in spots and the railroad that connected Humboldt with the Bay Area had been open less than a year. But it was Fortuna that my father chose as the place to make his fortune. Maybe the name was the reason. It was to be his "fortuna."

Meanwhile, my mother, Catherine (Caterina) Bertalino, was making her own way toward a new life in the United States, pointing also to San Francisco. She was born in 1892 and was just two years old when her father died. She grew up in Pont-Canavese with her mother and sister. They were closely associated with her mother's family, the Valerios. In 1916, in her early 20s, my mother emigrated directly to San Francisco to join the family of her uncle, Vittorio Valerio, his wife, Virginia, and their three sons.

My parents met in 1918 at a party in San Francisco given by her aunt and uncle. World War I had just ended and my father, who had left the bakery in his cousin's care and joined the Army in 1917, had just returned from France, where he served with the 91st division of the 363rd Infantry. This division, being substantially from San Francisco and Northern California, was recognized as San Francisco's own and received a heroes' homecoming, with parades and celebrations. The 91st was involved in many of the battles of World War I, including those that occurred in Meuse-Argonne, Ypres-Lys and Saint-Mihiel.

With his bakery experience, my father was assigned as a cook for Company C. One of the war experiences he told me about was how he and two others hauled a wagon full of food to soldiers at the front line, under very dangerous conditions. For this he received the Croix de Guerre from the Belgian government. His war exploits were written up in the *Fortuna Beacon*, making him something of a local hero.

After his safe return, after that party at Valerios, my father returned to Fortuna and the bakery. But he and my mother kept up a steady flow of letters – until my dad proposed. They were married in San Francisco in 1919.

Fortuna must have been a shock to my mother. Her three- year "Americanization" in San Francisco had been something of a social whirl, certainly with enough parties and music and dances to keep a young woman busy. So, when she moved north as a bride, to live in a tiny apartment above the bakery, it was a dramatic – I might even say it was a traumatic – transition from that very active North Beach community. And, needless to say, it was much different than the village life in Italy.

In later life, she didn't hesitate to admit that Fortuna was not her cup of tea. There were no friends to visit with. The second-floor living quarters were pretty much her world and I'm sure she was lonely. Her only activities were keeping house and attending to the needs of my father, who worked from 4 a.m. to the middle of the afternoon in the bakery below. Her "duties" were expanded considerably on June 11, 1920, when I was born, in the apartment above the bakery. My mother was attended by her aunt, Virginia Valerio, who came from the Bay Area for the occasion.

From the moment of my birth, of course, I completely occupied her attention. My baby pictures and posed childhood photographs show that I was very special in her eyes.

In the Twenties, everyone dressed well for any occasion, even in rural Humboldt. Men wore suits with vests and hats outside the home or workplace. No one ever went to church without the proper attire. And my mother saw to it that I was outfitted in high style. My hair, which was thick and curly, was always neatly combed. Family photos show that I was a good-looking kid.

My earliest memories are of my father's bakery. Our living quarters above it, where I was born, were very small, so cramped for space that I spent much of my childhood downstairs in the bakery. I learned to stay out of the way, do what I was told and appreciate the camaraderie and working relationships of my father, his cousin and the men and women who worked for them.

When I was 12 years old, I was given my first bakery job. I would report, without fail, early in the morning, before school – to open and close the ovens. The bakery's large brick ovens were 20 feet by 10 feet in size. Every morning, they were fired with diesel burners. To preserve the right temperature inside the oven, the doors had to be opened and closed very quickly. For a baker working alone, this was nearly impossible, since it involved several steps.

So my very important job was to stand by the door when the baker was ready to insert the giant spatula holding the loaves of unbaked dough, open it on command, and close it quickly. The baker could put from six to ten loaves into the oven – or take them out – in less than a minute. With my help. In hindsight, I suspect this "important job" was a diversion, preventing possible mischief in a busy baking area. I certainly don't remember feeling important at the time. Nor do I remember whether I enjoyed the job or hated it. I was just where I was supposed to be.

These were the Depression Years, the early 1930s. And it was the second time around for my family in the bakery business in Fortuna, a small town in Humboldt County in rural Northern California. The family journey that brought us back to Fortuna is an important part of my story. It is one of those immigrant stories that make America so interesting – and so great.

My parents' life in Fortuna revolved exclusively around the bakery and a few Italian families, some of them relatives. Driving out to the redwoods on Sunday was a real treat. And we managed to squeeze out a week in the summer to go to Berkeley and San Francisco where we would always visit the Valerios. "Barba" and

"Mania" – which mean uncle and aunt in the Piemontese dialect – were like grandparents to me. Their three sons, Frank and twins Louis and John, were like my uncles. My parents gave me my middle name after the oldest, Frank.

Like so many of the immigrant generations, my father worked hard and lived very frugally, and, by 1926, had accumulated enough savings and investments to retire. He sold his interest in the bakery to his cousin and partner, James Camerlo, and the family moved back to the Bay Area. My parents purchased a lot on Parker Street in Berkeley where they built a modest two-story house just three blocks from the Valerios and near other close friends. Selling their business and retiring in their 30s, they were young enough to fully enjoy the social life of Berkeley, which, I'm sure, delighted my mother after the confining years in Fortuna. Now my father's weekday routine was to commute to San Francisco by train and ferry. He would spend the morning at the office of his broker, studying the stock market and making investments with margin accounts, which was the financial custom of those wildly prosperous times. When the markets closed in the East, he would, like many other investors, spend the rest of the day visiting friends, playing bocce ball and enjoying his garden.

As for my six-year-old self, I became a "city kid" with no hesitation. I attended Longfellow Grammar School in Berkeley where I found many playmates and readily accepted the urban advantages, like San Pablo Park, near my home, and outings to Neptune Beach in Alameda.

I can't recall what it was that first attracted me to the violin, but I began asking my parents to let me learn to play. They thought I was too young but I guess I wore them down, because, by the time I was eight they had given me a beginner-size violin and I was taking weekly lessons in our home from Miss Georgia Bliss. I still can feel, keenly, her exasperation when she would discover I had neglected to practice during the week.

The violin also caused some of my schoolmates to tease me whenever I packed it back and forth to school to play with others in the music class. Fortunately, I was not easily dissuaded because

~ 20 ~

my violin brought me a great deal of enjoyment in later years.

Then came the family financial crisis that occurred with the stock market crash and ensuing panic in the fall of 1929. Stock prices dropped precipitously and margin accounts were called.

My father took serious losses in his portfolio. To recover, he negotiated an arrangement with his cousin and reacquired his interest in the Fortuna Bakery. In 1931, he returned to Humboldt. The rest of the family, now including my sister, Rosemarie, who was born in 1930, stayed in Berkeley for a time. ❖❖❖

CHAPTER II ~ TEENAGE YEARS

In 1932, my father came back to Berkeley to move the family to Fortuna. He arranged for a van to ship our furnishings north and the Berkeley house was rented for $35 a month. It's safe to say that my father's financial woes in the Great Depression had a distinct impact on my own business plans. I resolved, early on, never to make financial decisions that might impact my family's standard of living. And I never have.

I'm sure that my mother despaired at the return to Fortuna. She would later suggest that she thought it was like being sent back to jail. But I was a sturdy 12-year-old and I welcomed the change. I have always considered that growing up in Fortuna was a great blessing.

I enrolled in the eighth grade at the grammar school – there was only one – and soon made many friends among my classmates, friendships firm enough to last for generations. Even now, several of us find occasions to get together. Our teacher was a stern maiden lady, Miss Louise Herman. We called her "Biddy" behind her back. During penmanship hour, she would walk up and down the aisles, watching all 30 of us, observing and making suggestions. Penmanship training was in pen and ink. We dipped the pen into the small inkwell and applied it to the paper until the ink was consumed.

"Biddy" Herman wore the same grey uniform dress every day. And it was frequently covered with ink stains. In fact, she was known to wonder aloud why her dress was always splattered with ink after penmanship class, when she wasn't using a pen. Then, one day as she walked by, she caught sight of my classmate Elmer Johnson dipping his pen in the ink and shaking the drops off the pen, aiming them to splash all over her dress. She was ready. When she caught Elmer in the act, she picked him up right out of his seat, shook him until his teeth rattled and packed him off to the principal's office. Discipline was swift and sure.

It was the custom for Fortuna High School to invite eighth

~ 22 ~

graders from district schools, from beyond Scotia in one direction to Bridgeville in the other, to a freshman dance and party to prepare them for the social aspects of high school life. For my friends and I this presented a real problem. None of us boys knew how to dance. The girls, on the other hand, had mastered the art.

In our retail bakery building on Main Street, which was separate from the bakery itself, the upper floor was vacant and available for social groups to use. So, after school, the girls taught the boys how to dance. We procured a phonograph and records and, after school, with a lot of missteps and giggling, we all became, if not accomplished, at least passable, fox-trotters and waltzers. When the "Freshman Prom" was held, we were ready.

Fortuna Union High School served all of the communities in central Humboldt County. Buses would bring in students from Carlotta in the east, Scotia and beyond to the south and Loleta in the north. During my four years, 1933-1937, approximately 500 students were enrolled. The school had a well-rounded curriculum with a complete music department, including an orchestra, band and chorus. The grading system was pass/fail. In retrospect, I can see that it lacked the competitive stimulation of a conventional grading system. The college preparatory curriculum was limited, while courses in welding, mechanics and agriculture abounded, reflecting the community it served. Of the 100 students in my class of 1937, few went to college – even fewer of us graduated from college.

Despite my expanding responsibilities in the bakery, I managed to participate in many school activities. Fortuna Union offered all sports activities, with the exception of football. In the late 1920s a student was severely injured and the sport had been abandoned. My sport was track. I won medals at the meets held with all the high schools in Southern Humboldt County. My banner year was in 1936, when I broke the county record for the 100-yard dash and the 220-yard dash, and was anchorman during the record-breaking relay race.

I played violin in the orchestra and learned to play the trumpet in the marching band. As a junior, I was selected to join the All-Northern California Young Musicians organization. We spent a week in San Francisco in a concert program conducted by Alfred (Papa) Hertz, the director of the San Francisco Symphony. In 1937, with the financial assistance of the Fortuna Rotary Club, the marching band participated in the opening ceremonies of the Golden Gate Bridge.

In 1987, I financed the Fortuna High marching band's participation in the 50-year anniversary celebration of the bridge opening. As a thank-you, they invited me to march beside them, but the unexpected crush of people who jammed the bridge for the occasion ended any thought of an organized march and, in fact, stopped me from joining them because I was caught in the crowd attempting to get on the bridge.

During my junior and senior years, under the guidance of our music instructor, Lloyd Anderson, we organized a seven-piece western "cowboy" band. We called ourselves the Northwest Night Riders. We performed for anyone who would invite us, which included numerous community groups. We even performed on the grandstand at the Fortuna Rodeo, an event that drew participants from all over the West each summer. Lloyd Anderson also arranged for the Night Riders to "go on tour" to Los Angeles. We played at the Los Angeles Rotary Club, and entertained passengers on the train from Fortuna to San Francisco, then from San Francisco to Los Angeles.

Actually, I was, you might say, "in demand" as a musician in Fortuna. I often played violin at funeral services in the mortuary, which was on the same block as our bakery, and "Taps" on my trumpet at services for veterans of World War I. I usually practiced the violin in my bedroom in our apartment above the bakery. One building removed was the town's only post office. Since there was no home delivery, residents would come to the post office for their mail daily.

One day I happened to be on the corner outside of our building when an elderly man approached me. Conservatively dressed with a long beard, he reminded me of one of the Smith Brothers on the cough drop packages. In a soft voice he asked if I was the one playing the violin that he could hear coming from the building next door. I told him I was. He explained that he had an extra violin and asked me if I would like to try it. He brought it to me the next day.

I liked it immediately. Its tone quality greatly exceeded that of my own violin. In the cowboy band and in a small orchestra dance band we put together, my violin was often drowned out by the brass instruments. I told him I thought his violin would give me better presence. He sold me that violin for $20. I remember my mother would always say to me, "You must save money for a rainy day," but I spent it all on that violin.

At our graduation, I performed a solo, playing Franz Liszt's "Liebestraum." I think it went pretty well, but I also recall that, afterwards, my mother scolded me for using a music stand to read the music. She was sure – and I think she was right – that I would have done equally well by memory.

I used the new violin in high school and through college, until it ended up in the closet, unused. Later, I discovered that William Notley, the retired rancher who sold me the violin, was the "fiddler" grandfather of Gaye LeBaron, columnist for years with the Santa Rosa Press Democrat.

Once, in the 1990s, when I was reminiscing with Gaye about our mutual Humboldt County roots, I was remembering the old gentleman who sold me the violin and she mentioned that her grandson had expressed interest in learning to play. At a gathering in 2001, I gave the violin to her for her grandson and asked her to tell him the story and special history of his great grandfather's violin.

Years later, Gaye told me that David McCarroll, a highly accomplished violinist friend, had borrowed the instrument for a concert tour of Southeast Asia and had insured it for $15,000. She offered to return it. Of course, I said no. At last report her 17-year-old grandson was playing the family violin in Berkeley's Young People's Symphony Orchestra. It is back in the place where I began my lessons.

In my junior year, I was class president but when I ran for student body president, I lost to Clyde Williams, also a member of the Northwest Night Riders. In 1923, before the Depression, my father had purchased a Studebaker touring sedan. This was a big, high-priced ($2,300) acquisition. It was used as the family car through the years until 1935, when he purchased a new Dodge sedan.

Cars in those days, at least our Dodge, did not have automatic windows, radio, air conditioning or even a heating system. Yet, to us, it was a state-of-the-art automobile. On acquiring the Dodge, my father gave me the Studebaker. During my junior and senior years my friends and I had the luxury of a roomy sedan for our high school adventures.

Fortuna, with mountains and forests and the rivers around it, was a wonderful place to grow up, not only sporting around in the Studebaker, but also fishing for the then plentiful trout, steelhead and salmon in the Eel and Van Duzen rivers and hunting in the hills. My father was not a hunter but friends of his took me hunting. I remember an expedition to adjoining Trinity County where I shot my first deer at age 14. And I was the only one in the group of men who got a buck on that trip. A proud moment.

All through my school years I continued my work at the family bakery. As time went by, I graduated from the early-morning ovens to the wrapping and slicing machines. I worked in the summers and after school and even at recesses and noon hours. Because the school was close by, I worked just about any time I was not in classes.

I also took trays of pastries and cakes from the bakery to our retail store on Main Street, and by the time I was 15, I was tending the retail store after 4:30 p.m., which was the time our sales lady, "Effie" Rawley, had to leave. Then there was the matter of finding bananas. One of the very popular pies made by Stein, our Norwegian pastry baker, was an absolutely amazing banana cream pie. In order to acquire the necessary bananas, I would scour the stores in Fortuna, buying every banana they had, and often being given bananas too ripe to sell. The over-ripe ones provided the best banana flavor to the custard cream. I had my driver's license at 15 and made deliveries to stores as far away as Carlotta on the Van Duzen River, Loleta out towards Eureka, and to various dairies and ranches which were some of our best customers.

During 1937-1938, the price for a loaf of bread was 10 cents retail, eight cents wholesale. Day-old bread at the bakery sold for five cents. The going wage was 25 cents an hour. The Pacific Lumber Company in nearby Scotia owned not only the lumber company, but also all the houses, the company store and the hotel. To sustain employees who needed additional funds, or those employed only during seasonal periods, the company issued "Scotia Scrip." The scrip became an acceptable medium of exchange for several of the retailers in the towns surrounding Scotia. At the bakery, scrip was accepted. When enough had been accumulated we would go to the company store in Scotia and purchase sugar, shortening or other ingredients the bakery could use.

During this time, unemployment was severe. Transients came by the bakery asking if they could work for a "little tuppence." My father never refused them. Our floor would be swept as often as they came by, as many as four or five times a day. When sacks of old bread accumulated, my father arranged with a rancher friend to regularly pick up the sacks. The old bread made good cattle feed. In return, the rancher would give my father a butchered pig or calf.

After graduation, I worked at the bakery making deliveries to our wholesale customers – stores, restaurants and lumber camps in the several communities in central Humboldt County. I have happy memories of driving the bakery's panel truck around the county – and a not-so-happy recollection of the time I put it into a ditch with a wedding cake I was delivering to a reception in the back. Fortunately, there was time to make another, but I felt terrible that I had caused the pastry man to be called back to work after his long night shift.

By the end of summer, I intended to go to Humboldt State College with three friends. But there was no one available to make the routes to the stores. With a nationwide depression in full force, I needed to remain with the bakery. As an alternative to attending school, I took correspondence courses through the University of California, Extension Division.Then, in December of 1937, we found a young man who would take my place at the bakery. I was free to go to college.

I decided to attend the University of San Francisco. As I was saying goodbye to my father, I knew I would not be returning until May or June. My departure was dramatic. I thought it must be like the farewells of the young people leaving their home in Italy, not knowing if or when they would ever return – and some never did. It definitely felt like a turning point in my life.

I shook my father's hand. Men never, ever, embraced in those days. And he said something I have never forgotten. "Don't worry about me, but remember you have a mother and sister." The baton of responsibility had been passed. I took my responsibility very seriously and carried that "baton" until they died – my mother in 1975, my sister in 2008.

Looking back, I think that was the day I grew up. ❖❖❖

CHAPTER III ~ COLLEGE YEARS

My first attempt at higher education didn't go too well. During my one semester at the University of San Francisco, I stayed with the Valerios at their home in Berkeley. Commuting to USF, located in central San Francisco, required a streetcar to the ferry, then a trip on the ferry, then another streetcar to the campus. I had a class three days a week in religion that started at 8 a.m. I rose at 5 a.m., caught the streetcar by 6 a.m. and was at school by 8 a.m. Additionally, I signed up for the Reserve Officers' Training Corps, which, on occasion, required drill until the very late afternoon.

I was busy, the days were long and, in spite of the fine treatment I received at USF and the friends I made, I was one homesick boy of 17. I had been advanced a year in grammar school and was a year younger than most of my classmates, which had never seemed a problem in high school, but on this bigger stage I felt young. In addition, I was hearing from my Fortuna friends who had gone to Humboldt State College, telling me what an enjoyable time they were having. Compared to my own situation, with no campus life, living miles from campus, attendance at Humboldt State became very appealing.

I returned to Fortuna in May of 1938 and resumed my work at the bakery for the summer. My primary work was the daily delivery and sales to resort areas on the Van Duzen and Eel rivers. In August, I applied for enrollment at Humboldt State College. (The college has since become a university.) The enrollment at Humboldt was approximately 450 students. We had a well-rounded faculty of conscientious professors. Classes were small and rapport between professors and students was excellent.

My first year, I roomed at a boarding house called Elmores', the name of the family that owned the house. My roommate was Glen Goble. We became and remained close friends until his premature death in 1975. My second year at Humboldt State, Glen, his cousin Ivan Olsen and I rented a small apartment within walking distance of the campus for $30 a month. We prepared our own meals. With what I brought from the bakery and food from Ivan's parents' ranch in Ferndale, we lived well – and very inexpensively. Already, there were signs of the coming war. Italians in America watched Benito Mussolini, the head of the totalitarian Italian government, as he took wrong turns. Rather than remaining neutral or joining the Allied interests, he sided with Adolph Hitler. This was a grave error, causing general regret. Up to then, Mussolini had actually formalized some very constructive moves in Italy. Unfortunately, joining the Axis Powers brought Italy severe hardships during the war years. Mussolini and his mistress ended up hanging by their heels from a tree, executed by Italian nationalists.

Here in the United States, the federal government was developing a civilian pilot training program. Qualified young men were given flying lessons and flight training. Humboldt State's quota for training was 10 men. I applied and was accepted, subject to a physical examination. I saw an optometrist in Eureka for the eye exam, hoping for the required 20/20 in both eyes. The optometrist found that I had 20/20 vision in my right eye, but my left eye, with astigmatism, was just 20/15.

I was greatly disappointed. I remember overhearing the attending junior doctor suggesting to the senior doctor in the adjoining room that I should be passed. But the senior doctor would not agree and my application was accordingly denied.

This was a great disappointment, particularly when the 10 student pilots became Big Men on Campus, idolized by the student body. Later, I would see it differently. Four of the 10 were killed in the war.

One of my sources of income during college, besides the $50 a month my father gave me, was working part time at the Safeway store in Eureka, which was managed by John Sandretto. John was the oldest son of Dominic Sandretto, my father's cousin and the shoemaker in Fortuna. John's brother, Amadeo, and I were close friends at Humboldt State. Thanks to John's generosity, we both worked at the Safeway store. I worked mainly in the produce department. The assistant manager demanded that we be active at all times. So when we were not waiting on customers, we were to sweep the floor or sprinkle water on the green vegetables so they would remain fresh.

My other source of income was as Business Manager of the Humboldt State yearbook. This involved contacting local merchants and professional people in Arcata and Eureka and asking them to place ads of varying size in the yearbook. For this, I received 20 percent of the price of the ad. I have often thought that this experience dealing with the public, along with my experience in the bakery, was very effective training for my coming business career.

After my second year at Humboldt, Amadeo and I decided to enroll at the University of California at Berkeley. After the summer months, when I again worked a delivery route for the bakery, we left for Berkeley. We were able to find a very modest ground-floor apartment on Piedmont Avenue close to the campus. Our third roommate was a close friend, Bob Cort, whom I met at University of San Francisco. My major was Business Administration. Amadee, as my cousin was called, majored in sciences and Bob in social studies. Bob subsequently became a lawyer in San Francisco.

I was very conscientious about earning good grades. I felt that my two years at Humboldt had been beneficial mostly for the social aspects of campus life. Studying never came easily to me. Amadee, on the other hand, was casual to the point of negligence, except on the night before an examination. He would study mostly in bed and get a high grade the next day, generally an A. I envied him, but I guess learning easily wasn't a family trait.

One of my sources of income at Berkeley was with Philip Morris cigarettes. The placement agency at the university sent me to Philip Morris because the company was seeking a limited number of students who would circulate among the fraternity and sorority houses and boarding houses. We were to pass out small boxes of two cigarettes each to the students. Smoking, in those days, was very proper and popular. Consequently, sorority houses and fraternity houses were very cooperative in allowing me to give my sales pitch on the benefits of Philip Morris cigarettes as opposed to other popular brands, such as Camels and Lucky Strike. Cigarettes were 15 cents a pack. Military personnel could purchase them for as low as 5 cents a pack. Many people who became addicted smoked as much as two to three packs a day.

My remuneration for this work was about $300 a month, a considerable sum. When the spring semester was about to end, I prevailed upon the Philip Morris representative to allow me to continue working during the summer months in Fortuna. He agreed. Since my potential contacts were limited compared to Berkeley, a number of my cigarette-smoking friends were amply supplied. I myself was a moderate smoker, generally smoking one or two cigarettes during the cocktail hour.

During the first year that Amadee, Bob and I roomed together, the draft became effective. At first, students were liberally deferred. In the spring of 1940, the Navy and Army air corps began recruiting men for pilot training. Amadee decided he wanted to join. One of the physical requirements was a minimum height of 5'6". Amadee was a freckle under this requirement. Because we believed – I'm not sure why – that a person is somewhat taller in the morning than later in the day, on the morning of Amadee's exam Bob and I had him lie on the floor. Bob pulled from the head. I pulled from the feet. After a few minutes of this "therapy," Amadee dressed and went over to the recruiting office in San Francisco. He passed the examination.

Amadee was sent to the naval flight-training program in Corpus Christi, Texas. He passed the entire test and became a second lieutenant in the Marine Corps. Later he became a dive-bomber, as distinguished from a fighter pilot. He was assigned to a squadron in the Pacific and was in the early battles of Guadalcanal. This was a very bleak period for the war in the Pacific. According to one of his fellow pilots, Amadee was on his last flight mission before going on leave to Australia. The flight group encountered a Japanese transport. None of the pilots in the attack on the ship saw what happened to him. But Amadee never returned. He was declared Missing in Action in November of 1942.

Another member of his Squadron 141 was Dante Benedetti,

older brother of Gene Benedetti, who would become a Sonoma County friend. At the time I attended the University of San Francisco, Dante (Dan) was student body president. An exceptionally handsome young man, he was loved deeply by his family. Dan had been active in the Guadalcanal battles for 14 days when he was killed in action. To the Benedetti family, it was an inconceivable loss. His parents suffered for the remainder of their lives. Several members of the family have used the given name Dan since their loss.

During my final semester at Berkeley I encountered many challenges. I was able to secure residence at the International House. This prestigious facility on Piedmont Avenue in Berkeley where foreign students had living quarters was more like a hotel than a fraternity or boarding house. I had my own private room. Food was served in a cafeteria, with generous choices available. My school courses were the general requirements for a degree in Business Administration: economic theory, labor economics, marketing. In September, I was told I had been nominated for membership in the Beta Gamma Sigma Scholarship Society. This was a real honor, comparable to membership in Phi Beta Kappa, but in the Department of Economics.

Campus life in Berkeley was far different from Humboldt State. Humboldt was to Berkeley what living in Fortuna was to living in San Francisco. Close relations between students and faculty at Humboldt, with classes of 15 to never more than 30, were a dream compared to Berkeley's crowded lecture halls. Basic undergraduate classes required at Berkeley, including Economics 1A and Social Studies, had hundreds in attendance. Contact with professors was remote – often through one of their assistants.

Teaching assistants were usually graduate students, majoring in a similar area of study. Attending class could be augmented by buying "Phy-bate" notes, available for sale at the bookstore for the specific days of lecture. On occasion there were rallies and gatherings at Sather Gate by students expounding a particular cause. The clock mounted in the Campanile, a prominent tower located in the center of campus and visible throughout the San

~ 33 ~

Francisco Bay Area, sounded out the hours of the day. On occasion, generally late in the afternoon, it would play organ music. On the morning of the week beginning final examinations it would play "They're Hanging Danny Deever in the Morning." Someone had started the tradition as a humorous way of consoling students preparing and studying for their final examinations. Big Game Night, before the Stanford-Cal football game, was an occasion for rallies and bonfires and, of course, fraternity house parties to celebrate school spirit.

My own interests focused on my studies. I did participate in the symphony orchestra. I was second violin, which I took to be a good reflection of my ability in relation to the other string players, although professional musicians will tell you that second violin is simply another part of the music and not a reflection of skill. In retrospect, I have often evaluated how my college years related to my good fortune in the corporate world and its institutions. In those years, before we knew what an MBA was, a college degree was not essential for success in private enterprise. But it certainly didn't hurt. My last final examination, in Labor Economics, was on December 8, 1941. It was the culmination of my business education at Berkeley.

In ordinary times, I would have immediately started seeking employment in my chosen career along with other graduates. But the attack on Pearl Harbor, which occurred on the day before my last final, and the subsequent declaration of war changed all that. Many graduates enlisted immediately in the branch of the service of their choice. The alternative was to be drafted. Draftees were placed in a category of strongest need, usually the Army. Since I had attended only one semester of Reserve Officers Training Corps (ROTC) at the University of San Francisco, I thought I would probably duplicate my father's experience and be drafted into the infantry as a buck private. However, I learned that the Navy Supply Corps was seeking qualified candidates from the universities for their officer training program.

My draft board in Fortuna advised me of my 1A status. That meant I could and probably would be summoned for immediate conscription in the Army. I applied for a commission in the U.S. Navy Supply Corps and requested a deferment from the draft board in Fortuna, which it granted. The Navy indicated that its acknowledgement of my acceptance might take several weeks. So I was free to seek interim employment. My first position was as a clerk in the Department of Motor Vehicles in Oakland. My salary was $90 a month.

Then, after approximately two weeks, I learned that the Kaiser-Bechtel ship building collaboration in Richmond was hiring office staff. I was given a job in the accounting office, reviewing and authorizing expenditures for non-ship equipment needed in the shipyard. During these months, I had a room in the Berkeley home of my great aunt and uncle, the Valerios.

One Sunday morning in May, several weeks after I applied for the Supply Corps commission, my cousin Johnny Valerio came into my room. He lived a block away from his parents. I had given his address in my application to the Navy. I recall him saying that Sunday morning, "Now relax, but here's a letter from the Navy." At that moment, before opening the envelope, my heart was racing. Would it be acceptance or rejection?

Acceptance! My exuberance was immense. My instructions were to report to the officer in charge at the Naval Supply Depot in Oakland. I was to purchase the necessary uniforms of a naval officer, with the exalted rank of ensign, in preparation for induction. I terminated my position at the shipyards and found a store in Oakland that specialized in officers' uniforms, both formal blue and khaki. Then, properly dressed, but knowing nothing about the Navy, I proceeded by bus to the Naval Supply Depot and was directed to the office of the Senior Supply Officer, a Commander Ryan.

I introduced myself to his secretary and she invited me to sit down in a chair close to the commander's office. I could see him as she said, "The commander will see you in a few minutes." He saw me, all right, but it was a full two hours before he motioned me to come into his office. Apparently he had a very real disdain for young men coming directly out of college, already commissioned

~ 35 ~

as officers. He considered it an affront, after all the work he had put in to achieve his rank.

As I came in, standing in front of his desk, he looked up over his glasses and said, "Swear?" I thought for a moment, then replied, "Only when I get a little mad."

"No!" he said, "I don't mean that. I mean, do you swear to uphold the traditions of the U.S. Navy?" or words to that effect.

I promptly responded, "Oh, yes, sir!" ❖❖❖

CHAPTER IV ~ NAVY YEARS (1942-1945)

Now I was a probationary ensign in the Supply Corps, United States Naval Reserve. Losing that "probationary" adjective involved passing the required courses at the Harvard University graduate school in Cambridge, Massachusetts. The pressure was immense. Failing the class and not receiving my commission as a naval officer was the last thing I wanted my friends and relations to hear. I could only imagine how embarrassed I would be, having paraded around Fortuna in an ensign's uniform – not to mention the draft that awaited me and the very real possibility of being a buck private in the infantry.

In November of 1942, before Harvard, I was assigned to the interim processing area at the Oakland naval supply depot where newly received equipment was stored – actually simply spread across the floor in an enormous warehouse. All Naval supply depots were supervised and operated by civil service personnel, with naval officers in strategic oversight positions. I had been in this temporary "strategic oversight" role for about a week when I encountered Commander "Bull" Durham. Commander Durham was the officer in charge. His nickname may have come from the popular brand of tobacco. Or it may have been because of his appearance and his general demeanor.

As he approached, I saluted promptly and stood quietly alert. He glared at me and gave me a sloppy wave of his hand. I started walking. I was maybe 10 yards beyond him when he spotted a container that was covered with dust. It had obviously been there for a long time. He brushed the dust off the receiving ticket and saw that the container was a box of spark plugs for Pratt & Whitney engines, parts in short supply and great demand at airfields throughout the Pacific.

Commander Durham assumed that I was the one to blame for failing to deliver the spark plugs. He stopped me, berated me, walked away, turned around and laid into me again. It was the worst chewing out in the duration of my Navy service. Maybe of my

~ 37 ~

life. I just stood there, speechless, as visions of an abrupt end to my naval career passed before my eyes. But he walked on. I went in the opposite direction. I was in Oakland less than a month and, thankfully, had no more meetings with Commander Durham.

My classes at Harvard's Graduate School started the week after Thanksgiving, 1942. Regularly scheduled cross-country flight service was still in the future, so I made the trip by train, which took three days and two nights through exceptionally severe winter weather. I have thought often about our arrival – on November 27, 1942 – and how many fates turned on what happened the night we checked into our rooms in Hamilton Hall.

The military class ahead of ours, 300 strong, was standing in formation, by companies, in the square in front of the dormitory as we arrived. Coming from all parts of the country, many of the new men were unaware that blackout rules were in effect on the East Coast as well as the western states. By 6 p.m., with the senior men still at muster, the lights remained on in some of the rooms and the men in the yard began to holler, "Turn them off! Turn them off!" The lights went out. But, next morning, the officer in charge declared that the yelling constituted disorderly conduct and ordered all members of the senior class confined to their quarters at 9 p.m. It was a Saturday night.

As it happened, their un-military behavior saved them a date with history – and may have saved their lives. That was the night 100 people died at the Cocoanut Grove, a Boston nightclub favored by the Harvard crowd. The club was in rooms below street level with only one stairway out. The fire caught draperies ablaze, creating toxic fumes that caused a panic. It was a fire that attracted national attention. We all had phone calls from worried families the next day. The tragedy changed the codes of fire safety everywhere. Had there not been a 9 p.m. curfew, many in that "disorderly" senior class would have been in the popular nightclub.

My roommates and I were not on restriction and had gone off to see the town. We were on our way to the Cocoanut Grove but, fortunately, we stopped for a drink at another Boston landmark called Dinty Moore's. We arrived at the ill-fated nightclub just as

~ 38 ~

emergency crews were carrying the victims out to ambulances lined up on the street.

The Harvard dormitory quarters consisted of two rooms joined by a sitting room, two men to a room, assigned alphabetically. My roommates were Thompson, Thompson and Trimbel. We all lived with the threat of revocation of our commission should we fail our classes. This fear proved a strong incentive for all of us to study as hard as we could. Although studying never came easily to me, I finished the course in the upper 10 percent of my class.

The Navy, concerned about a shortage of junior officers in the fleet, asked for volunteers for early assignment. I stepped up and, with about 20 others, finished the courses in February instead of May, when the group was assigned to Seabee Construction Battalion Center at Quantico, Virginia, a base readying Seabees for the Pacific Theater.

I didn't go to Quantico. Instead, I was ordered to a destroyer base in San Diego, where I was to be assistant supply officer on a submarine tender headed for Perth, Australia – when the ship was ready.

The senior supply officer there was Lawton Shurtliff, who, at this writing, is something of a neighbor, living on Chalk Hill Road near Healdsburg. From time to time, even though it's been 68 years since we served together in the Navy, I will call him and say, "Ensign Trione reporting for duty, sir."

I spent a month at trivial tasks at the San Diego base, waiting for the ship to be completed. I also dated the daughter of Captain Sackett, the supply officer who was my immediate superior. I escorted her to a base function and, shortly thereafter, I was surprised to receive new orders directing me to the 13th Naval District in Seattle, Washington. I was told I was going to a motor torpedo boat station, Base No. 5, on the island of Adak. Instead of heading south, I was going far north. I have always wondered if my dating the captain's daughter had anything to do with my being assigned to the Aleutian Islands.

I was flown, with 10 other officers, to Kodiak, Alaska, where I boarded a Navy troop ship destined for Dutch Harbor, then on to

Adak and Base No. 5. Motor torpedo boats, commonly known as PT boats (a U.S. hull classification symbol for "Patrol Torpedo"), were used by the Navy to attack larger surface ships. The PTs carried two to four torpedoes and counted on small size and high speed to close on their targets.

There were 531 PT boats built for the Navy at the start of WWII, of which 99 were lost. The PT squadrons operated from 88 locations – 25 main bases and 63 satellites – that stretched from the English Channel and the Mediterranean Sea to the most remote Pacific Islands. When the Japanese invaded the Aleutian Islands in 1942, the Navy sent several squadrons to four sites in the Aleutian Islands – Dutch Harbor and Finger Bay on Adak Island as well as Amchitka and Attu. I was assigned to the main base at Finger Bay.

The base was located on a remote part of the island, away from Massacre Bay where the airstrip and major naval facilities were located. The smaller Finger Bay provided barely adequate protection from the 100-knot winds known as "williwaws" blowing from the icy coast out across the Bering Sea. It was about an hour by boat from Finger Bay to Massacre Bay, most of it through open water. The Bering Sea temperature was so low that a person could live no more than 15 minutes in it. This estimate was never far from our minds, making that trip.

As commissary and dispersing officer, I was "lucky" enough to make the trip almost weekly. At Massacre Bay, I would order provisions and a substantial amount of cash for disbursement on paydays. The crews generally preferred cash, probably for psychological reasons, although many would request money orders for mailing to their dependents in the States.

Paper money wore out quickly on Adak. There was a fair amount of gambling, of course, and, as expected, there were the few card sharks with large sums to finance the next game. With all this circulation through the base between paydays, paper money got old and tattered, So part of my job was to change old U.S. currency for new, which required a visit, with an escort of enlisted men, to the main office at Massacre Bay.

~ 40 ~

This courier service went off without incident, but the ocean voyage to and from Massacre was another matter. I recall one trip with the base medical doctor, Mark Virnig. As we went out to sea from Finger Bay, we encountered very heavy winds. The boat we generally used was the captain's gig, a 25-foot inboard vessel. It was reasonably comfortable, although it was susceptible to extreme rolling in rough waters. At the helm was the coxswain, a man I knew to have been a barber from a small Midwestern town – far from any ocean.

On this especially memorable trip the swells caused by heavy winds rolled the gig hard from side to side. As we rode the swells, we needed to turn 90 degrees to the south to reach Massacre Bay. The turn would take the boat into heavy waves that could easily have capsized us. The coxswain, with his limited experience, was very hesitant to take the chance. Instead of turning, he held the course, taking us further and further out to sea, for what seemed like an eternity. Both the doctor and I became, shall we say, very concerned. I still recall hearing Dr. Virnig, a devout Catholic, murmuring his prayers as the boat pitched and rolled. Finally, at what seemed the last moment, the coxswain revved the motor and swung the boat into an abrupt 90-degree turn. We proceeded safely to Massacre Bay, much relieved.

While the sea voyage could be thrilling, the alternative route between the two bases was even more difficult. It was 10 miles across the island's rolling hills. Adak, like all the Aleutians, was completely treeless. The surface was tundra, which is like a soft carpet 12 to 18 inches thick. Walking on tundra is extremely difficult. The Bering Sea, therefore, was the transit of choice.

The U.S. military's presence in these remote islands began in the spring of 1943, when the joint forces of the Navy, Marine Corps and Army prepared to re-take Kiska and Attu islands, the only part of the U.S. that was occupied by the Japanese during WWII. The islands are at the extreme west end of the Aleutians. In preparation, a squadron of naval vessels – a carrier, cruiser, destroyer and two transport ships carrying an Army invasion force – headed for Attu, and, after several days of bombardment, the Army went ashore.

The May-June battle for Attu lasted 19 days and was not without cost. The American forces lost 549 men, with 1,100 wounded and 1,200 more suffering cold-related injuries because the American troops were ill equipped for the freezing weather. Attu would prove to be the only battle of the war fought on American soil. Or ice.

In August, when a similar invasion force went ashore at Kiska, after several days' bombardment, they found the island completely deserted. The Japanese, under heavy fog, had escaped. This discovery occasioned relief, but also some embarrassment to those who missed the evacuation completely and were caught by surprise.

Part of the challenge of being a commissary officer in the Aleutians was the on-going scarcity of fresh vegetables. Commissary headquarters was constantly challenged to provide the necessary vitamins – and some variety.

This was apparently what the headquarters had in mind when it ordered the avocados. They arrived, enough for the entire Alaska force, packed in flats of two dozen each, two flats to a box. The commissary HQ, unaware of the packing method, had ordered way more than they intended. They had also overestimated the demand. The personnel on the islands were from all over the country and many – perhaps, most – had never seen nor heard of, much less tasted, an avocado. Even if they recognized them, many had never learned to like them. The result was an enormous number of rapidly ripening avocados stored in the main commissary warehouse, with the need to distribute them growing more urgent every day.

The Orders of the Day, the newsletter distributed to all facilities, urged more consumption of avocados. The pressure was on the individual commissaries. One commissary officer with a sense of humor responded to the pressure by ordering boxes for the squadron making raids on Japanese-held territory. As they unloaded their bombs, they dropped avocados.

The threat of Japanese invasion via the Aleutian Islands had passed long before the "avocado drop." Tensions were easing a bit. In the South Pacific in June of '42, the Battle of Midway was a resounding success for our U.S. fleet. In effect, it marked the turning point of the war in the Pacific, ending the dominance of Japan's naval power.

Motor torpedo boat squadrons were assigned to bases in the South Pacific where Allied forces were re-taking the many Japanese-occupied islands. With the reduction of naval personnel, my responsibilities as a commissary and disbursing officer were eliminated, and I was assigned to the supply officer in command of the base at Massacre Bay.

Now monotony became the problem. Alcohol was prohibited to enlisted personnel, with the single exception of beer served on Saturday nights at the recreation hall. Officers, on the other hand, were given the opportunity of ordering one bottle a week of a whiskey of their choice, subject to availability. The ingenuity of some enlisted personnel became evident when they took the alcohol used in torpedoes and found ways to distill it to drinkability. These attempts were not always successful and some sailors ended up blind by drinking from a bad batch.

Terms of duty ranged in the Navy from one year to one and a half years. In the case of Army personnel, some were there for over two years without even the minimal comforts of the Navy base. There was a considerable amount of scheming to shorten the time and find a way home. One was pyorrhea. There were few if any dental facilities in the Alaskan command, and men with severe gum disease were often flown home. When word of this got around, the incidence of pyorrhea complaints increased alarmingly.

Meanwhile, I was promoted to lieutenant junior grade, which added a half-size stripe to my ensign's sleeve. And, to my great joy, I was sent to the 13th Naval District Headquarters in Seattle for reassignment. I was fortunate enough to land a berth on a freighter returning to Seattle. I occupied a pleasant officer's stateroom for the seven-day trip with stops in Dutch Harbor, Kodiak and Sitka. I don't remember much about the trip, except the unwavering food schedule: 6 a.m. breakfast, 10 a.m. juice and coffee, noon lunch, 3 p.m. snacks, 6 p.m. dinner, 10 p.m. snacks. It never varied. We arrived well fed. The captain aboard the freighter, whose name I have forgotten, was very friendly. Before we docked, I gave the young skipper my parka and other cold weather gear. It was much appreciated. And I was happy to be shed of it.

When I got to the destroyer base in Seattle, I found rooms in the Bachelor Officer Quarters at Sand Point Naval Air Station. I had received another promotion, to lieutenant senior grade, and awaited orders from the 13th Naval District. For many good reasons, I was hoping to avoid assignment to the South Pacific. I knew there was a motor torpedo boat base in Naples, Italy. And that obviously had much greater appeal. I forwarded my request through the proper authorities. Then, for the next two weeks, I waited. I had only to report in every morning. For the rest of the day I had plenty of time to ponder my fate.

Then one morning when I reported to district headquarters, I found my orders had arrived. As always, these moments make one's heart beat faster. I realized, whatever the assignment was, a change was coming that could radically alter my life. Imagine my surprise when I opened the sealed document and found I was to report to the supply officer in command at the Naval Air Station, Alameda, California. I was going home. My parents lived no more than 10 miles from the base.

Many on the staff at NAS Alameda were civil service personnel, especially those in the supply department. Naval officers were placed among the various divisions, in most cases alongside a civil service supervisor. I was assigned to be the receiving division officer in charge of the several receiving buildings.

The NAS Alameda was the main base for approximately nine auxiliary bases in the general area including, Monterey, Modesto, Merced, Crows Landing, one in Nevada and several to the north. They were all busy places in 1944 and '45. With the two full years of war behind us, the AOG section of the supply department, meaning Aircraft On Ground, was responsible for planes that were inoperable because of vital parts not immediately available.

~ 44 ~

Requests for these parts had priority, which meant we could circumvent the three to ten days ordinarily required to process new equipment into the official inventory.

When there was a critical part needed at an auxiliary base, a member of the department would deliver the item in person, invariably with a naval aircraft the size of which was determined by the size or number of items. There were 10 enlisted personnel in the AOG section, including civil service personnel. The person in charge, assigned as my assistant, was an enlisted WAVE – a very attractive and personable WAVE – named Madelyne V. Keyes.

Raised on a ranch in Arizona, she had enlisted in 1942, leaving a civil service job in Denver, Colorado. Her government work experience had earned her a storekeeper first class rating on her way to becoming a chief petty officer, which was the highest rank, next to warrant officer, for enlisted personnel. As I said, she was very attractive, but she was half an inch taller than I was. One day I summoned my courage and said, "If I were taller, I'd ask you for a date."

She didn't hesitate. "Don't let that stop you," she said. I didn't.

With auxiliary fields in places familiar to me like Santa Rosa and Arcata, I would manage to go on the special delivery runs whenever I could prudently spend the time. On some occasions, Madelyne and I would go together, flying off in Navy aircraft, on official duty. At the time, I was living at the Bachelor Officer Quarters on the base. Madelyne and three other WAVES had a nice apartment at the Hill Castle, a 12-story building close to Lake Merritt in Oakland.

One of my more interesting assignments was as chairman of the audit committee for the NAS Alameda Officers' Club. The club had excellent dining facilities, a cocktail bar and a room with about 50 slot machines. Among the patrons of the club, besides ships' companies, were the pilots of the many squadrons awaiting orders for some destination, usually the South Pacific. Being young and carefree with their funds, they fueled those slot machines, which made the club large profits. Fortunately, all profits were allocated to an enlisted personnel foundation.

The officer in charge of the Officers' Club was Charles Farrell, an actor who had been a matinee idol in an earlier era and would return to the profession after the war with the advent of television. He played Gale Storm's father in a popular show called "My Little Margie." To insure that my audit committee members were in an affable mood, he asked – and we readily agreed – that meetings be held during lunch, with whatever cocktails the committee members might wish. Consequently, the presentation of the statements for our perusal was generally unanimously accepted.

At Alameda, we felt a long way from the war, especially with the news of what was happening in the South Pacific. The operation at our base was almost like working in a civilian corporate operation. The work itself was painstakingly complex. In this period before computers or any form of information technology, keeping track of all the parts in the Navy's system was a difficult task. The nomenclature of airplane parts was different for different types of aircraft. And worse, the same part might have a different name in the military and civilian lists, or even in some Navy catalogs. Synchronizing the parts into the system required immense amounts of research and identification by a large staff of people.

The war ended in 1945. Germany surrendered in May, the Japanese in September, following the bombing of Hiroshima and Nagasaki. The process of delivering supplies to ships was now reversed. Carriers and supply ships began unloading their cargo on our piers. Not only aviation parts but also clothing and miscellaneous machinery and tools were literally dumped on the docks of the Naval Air Station with no identification. I was in charge of sorting out these supplies. The volume coming in was so overwhelming that we pitched two large circus tents for storage and identification. Marketable merchandise was sold to surplus stores at very low prices. Some of it was scrapped. Still more was stored in vacant buildings for possible future use.

At the Officers' Club, the large inventory of slot machines was declared illegal. They were taken by barge to the middle of San Francisco Bay and dumped.

Madelyne was transferred to the discharge base at Treasure Island. I remained on duty. On March 28, 1946, we were married at a ceremony in San Francisco with a reception at the Valerio home. So began my life with the wonderful woman who would be the mother of my sons and my companion for 56 years.

I had accumulated two months of leave time, so we enjoyed a leisurely honeymoon. We traveled in a 1932 Ford from San Francisco to Arizona to Mexico. Then we made our way to British Columbia, stopping along the way in Mount Vernon, Washington, where I was best man at my Fortuna friend Glen Goble's marriage to his wife, Barbara. In all, we logged more than 1,500 miles – without a spare tire!

Rentals were hard to find in the Bay Area in 1946. While we looked for an apartment, we lived with my parents in Berkeley. I spotted an ad in the Oakland Tribune for available apartments and decided to apply in person, in my uniform, at the Oakland office of Beckett & Federigi. The man at the desk was polite, but he warned me there was a waiting list of at least 30 applicants.

While I was waiting, a nice-looking man of my age came up and said hello. He had been a Navy aviator so we compared experiences for a few minutes. I found out later that, as he was leaving, he had spoken to Ted Conklin, the man who had taken my application, and told him, "Put his name on top of the list." He was C.C. "Bud" Dewitt, in charge of the mortgage lending division, which was the correspondent for the mortgage loan department of the New York Life Insurance Company.

Our brief chat must have impressed him. Within the week, I was advised that a four-room, ground floor apartment in a fourplex on 14th Avenue in Oakland was available. Thanks to Bud DeWitt, we had our first home. And, as later became apparent, I had made a valuable friend. ❖❖❖

PHOTOGRAPHS
Circa 1915 ~ 1964

My father's Fortuna Bakery in Humboldt County. I was born in the apartment on the second floor in 1920.

My mother, Catarina (Catherine) Bertalino, at age 23. before she came to the United States. 1915

My father, Vittorio (Victor) Trione, a private first class in the American army. He is wearing the Croix de Guerre awarded him by the Belgian government for service in World War I. 1918

Victor and Catherine's wedding portrait in San Francisco. 1919

I am going for a ride with my mother's twin cousins, Louie and John Valerio.
The twins, their parents and their older brother, Frank,
were our closest family. 1922

The Valerios. Left to right, John, my mother's Aunt Virginia,
Victor, Frank, my mother and Louis.

There was not a lot of traffic in Fortuna at the start of the 1920s.

At age 2, I didn't fully appreciate that the board sidewalks in Fortuna were made from heart redwood planks.

My mother saw to it that I was outfitted in high style.

Driving out to the redwoods on a Sunday in 1922 was a real treat for my father, my mother, and me.

My first Holy Communion, St. Joseph's Church, Fortuna. Circa 1926.

Fishing was not only fun but very, very productive in Humboldt County's Eel River in the early 1930s.

Fortuna's annual Rodeo Parade turned out a crowd. Our bakery entered with a loaf of bread longer than our bakery truck.

My trumpet and I pose, with Fortuna Union High School's band, on the steps of San Francisco's City Hall after marching across the Golden Gate Bridge on Opening Day in May of 1937. *(inset)* My high school graduation picture.

By 1939, I was firmly seated in my quest for higher education. With Doris Gunderson (*left*) and Rosie Ivansten (*right*), I am celebrating Barn Dance Day at Humboldt State College.
~ *Humboldt State University Library Archives*

My uniform and the ensign's stripe were both new in this photo. 1942

I'm an older, wiser Navy Lieutenant serving at Motor Torpedo Base #5 in the Aleutian Islands. 1943

Storekeeper 1st Class Madelyne Keyes, my aide at Alameda Naval Base. 1944

Madelyne and me on our wedding day, March 28, 1946.

The Trione family in 1946. To my right: Madelyne, my sister Rosemarie, my mother and my father.

My mother, father and me with baby Victor, in Berkeley in 1947.

With my boys, Victor and Mark, in Santa Rosa. 1949

With Mark and Victor in the yard of our first Santa Rosa house, on Finlaw Street. 1953

With Madelyne and our teenage sons on a camel tour of the Sphinx. 1964.

CHAPTER V ~ GETTING ON WITH BUSINESS

For many of us who served in the military, 1945 was a year of decision. With the war over, millions of young men and women were asked to choose between returning to civilian life or making a career of the armed forces. I applied for transfer from the naval reserves to regular Navy. As a lieutenant senior grade I was close to being eligible for promotion to lieutenant commander and my senior officer at the Alameda air station was encouraging me to stay on. My father was also urging me to stay with the Navy, seeing a bright and secure future for me and for my family.

My father was in poor health. He had sold his bakery in Fortuna and retired, once again, to Berkeley. I think he wanted to know that I was "settled." (He died three years later, in the week he turned 60 years old. At the time, heart bypass surgery was not available. I have often thought that if he could have survived another 10 years, surgery might have given him a chance at a longer, normal life.)

I was still pondering what decision to make on the July morning when I left our Oakland apartment to go to the 12th Naval District office in San Francisco. I thought about it on the train crossing the Bay Bridge and sat two more hours on a park bench, deliberating. Staying on active duty would involve transfers, some to sea, but all interesting. I would be eligible to retire at the ripe young age of 47. I could apply for a higher rank. But, as if some guiding force was directing me, I went into the office, went through the withdrawal procedure and became a 25- year-old veteran, abruptly unemployed – and looking for work.

Many veterans chose to go to the college or university of their choice, tuition paid by the government. But that did not interest me. I had my degree and I wanted to move directly into the work force. I assumed that my administrative experience in the Navy would give me an advantage in the job market. And, as a graduate of the University of California, I had access to a campus office that processed inquiries from businesses looking for employees.

~ 49 ~

The first job I selected, after weeks of checking and rechecking the list of opportunities, was with the Cleary Adding Machine Company. This was a new company that offered a type of adding machine with unique features. At a time when other companies were posting delays of up to a year for new machines, Cleary equipment was available for immediate delivery – a great selling point. The company was looking for young trainees who might qualify for future management opportunities, as the company planned to expand its marketing efforts nationwide.

Training consisted primarily of going to offices or stores and making "off the street" contacts. It served me well. I made over $1,000 a week, exceptionally good money at the time, but I didn't see it as my future.

So I was interested when I received a call from the University of California employment office indicating that a winery in Modesto wanted young men for training to become district sales managers. Perhaps it was my Northern Italian heritage, but for some reason the wine business seemed attractive, even though my knowledge of wine had been pretty much limited to watching my father produce what he was allowed for family use during Prohibition. The Modesto company was E. & J. Gallo Winery, owned and operated by brothers Ernest and Julio Gallo. I accepted the job.

Again, "training" consisted of so-called "cold calls," going store-to-store convincing owners to stock their shelves with Gallo. It wasn't an easy sell. Few grocery stores offered wine for sale and those that did had a very limited inventory. But I gave it my best, which apparently was noted. After three months on the job, the sales manager singled me out at a sales meeting. I still remember exactly what he told me.

"Trione," he said, "we are sending you to Atlanta, Georgia, where you will be our district representative for all the Southeastern United States." Flattering as the offer was, I declined. Atlanta was a long way from the Bay Area (not to mention Fortuna) in those pre-jet-travel times. I was newly married. We were planning a family. The thought of a cross-country move had no appeal. I decided to resign from Gallo and look elsewhere.

So I was back at the campus office, sorting through possibilities. I found that Prudential Insurance Company of America's mortgage loan department in San Francisco was seeking trainees for mortgage lending.

I applied and, after a thorough interview, I was accepted. The day I signed employment papers with Prudential I received a call from Ernie Gallo. He said, "I understand you are leaving the winery." I said I was and explained that leaving California was not what I wanted. He said, "Well, come to Modesto to the winery and we will work something out." To have the owner offer such an opportunity was overwhelming. But I reluctantly told him my decision had been made and I could not reverse it.

The Prudential position was an eight-to-five job in the San Francisco office where mortgage loan applications were processed, most of them for single-family homes. The more complex commercial loans went through another department. My job at Prudential was not what I had hoped. The office regimen and the paper shuffling weren't what this person, who had grown up in a family-owned business in very-rural Humboldt County, was looking for. It didn't take long for me to realize that some of the other employees had as much as 20 years of experience and were far more qualified than I would ever be. And they were still in the office every day, going over applications. I was purely miserable. I even thought of returning to the Navy. But I felt I had to live with the decisions I had made.

One day I accompanied one of the more experienced appraisers, Ray Mason, to a house in the Sunset District of San Francisco. It was to be the security on a mortgage loan. As we drove up to the house, a man was waiting for us in his car. After a brief greeting, he pointed out the house and left. We were to measure the outside of the house to determine its square footage. We would then describe the number of rooms, type of construction, and condition, and come to an estimate of the house's value relative to the amount of loan requested.

This was all recorded on a 10 x 12 inch worksheet, along with a sketch of the house and its layout. When all this was complete,

I noticed that Mason wrote on the edge of the sheet a name and a figure of 1½ percent. I asked him what it was. He said that was the fee the person would receive for directing the loan to us. That's when I realized that mortgage lending was a suitable profession for me, but I was on the wrong end of the operation. Producing mortgages from prospective borrowers was more to my liking than working for a company or institution that had the funding sources.

This was 1946. I attended a night school course on appraising techniques in San Francisco. I enlarged my limited knowledge of land values and appraising real estate. My interest, even then, was on single-family dwellings, rather than more complex evaluation procedures needed for commercial loans or multi-family apartment lending. It soon became apparent that I would have to make another change. On friendly terms, I parted company with the loan department of Prudential life insurance company. Fortunately, I had heeded my dear mother's advice: "You must save money for a rainy day." So Madelyne and I had enough to live conservatively for perhaps a year.

We had a comfortable place to live, thanks to C.C. "Bud" DeWitt, the Navy vet I had met in the Beckett & Federigi office when I was looking for a rental. DeWitt's help in getting us housing, I realized, had a profound effect on our destiny. If we hadn't found a place for ourselves in the war-crowded Bay Area, I would probably have re-enlisted and settled for a career in the Navy. In retrospect, it's clear that what I really wanted was to be independent. I wanted to work for myself, to use my skills in what I thought was the best way. Maybe it had to do with a family tradition, my forebearers owning their own businesses for generations. Whatever the reasons, I decided to trust myself. And I thought of that chance meeting with Bud DeWitt, who ran the mortgage lending company for Beckett & Federigi.

I thought perhaps I could become a loan solicitor for his firm. I got in touch him, learning that he had changed his company's name to East Bay Mortgage. He offered me the opportunity to work and for several months I sought out mortgage loans, mostly from

~ 52 ~

realtors in the area. A solicitor is paid strictly on a per transaction basis. There was enough activity that soon I was generating what I deemed an acceptable revenue stream.

Meanwhile our son Victor was born, in 1947, and I realized that, while soliciting mortgage loans gave me the independence I liked, it didn't provide the kind of security I felt my growing family needed. I knew that independence wasn't all I wanted. I wanted out of the city. I wanted to get back to Humboldt County. ❖❖❖

CHAPTER VI ~ SONOMA MORTGAGE

One day in 1947, I drove to Humboldt County to see what the prospects were. To give you an idea of my Spartan conservatism, rather than check into a motel, I left late in the afternoon from Oakland with my sleeping bag and I spent the night sleeping under the familiar redwoods of Richardson Grove State Park, near Garberville.

However, I found, to my disappointment, that opportunities for mortgage lending in Humboldt County were nil at the time. I did receive one lead. A realtor I talked with said an agent from Northwestern Mutual Life Insurance had contacted him for possible mortgage leads. When I returned to Oakland, I discovered that Northwestern Mutual had a loan office in San Francisco and I met with the manager, Harold Edelen. He said he thought Humboldt County was too remote for them. But, he said, "How about Sonoma County? Do you know of it?"

I said I knew it well, which was a distortion of the truth. My only contact with Sonoma County had been traveling through it, going back and forth for years, from Fortuna to the Bay Area. But I jumped at this chance. I made a cursory survey of Santa Rosa's mortgage prospects and found that Sonoma County was ripe for development, situated on the northern fringe of the Bay Area's war-time population boom, with affordable land and plenty of redwood lumber available for building.

I arranged to meet with Edelen and one of his staff in Santa Rosa. Again, I was impressed with Edelen. Subsequently we became good friends. After a follow-up meeting with the Milwaukee home office loan administrator, Karl Meier, Northwestern Mutual agreed to designate me their loan agent in Sonoma County, which included the communities of Petaluma, Sonoma, Sebastopol and Healdsburg.

This was the start of Sonoma Mortgage Corporation (SMC), although the name of my company, for the first year or two, was Sonoma Property Loan Company. I chose that because, as strange as it seems now, the word "mortgage" still had a negative connotation at the time. Older people, particularly, felt it indicated that they were debtors.

As a loan agent, I was paid strictly on a fee basis, but Northwestern's arrangement was very attractive. The going interest rate for home loans they were quoting was 4 percent. For each loan I originated, I received a 2 ½ percent one-time fee. Since the going rate in Sonoma County by all lenders, banks, savings and loans and private moneylenders was 6 percent, the opportunity was there for the taking. I was not at all popular with any of the local bankers.

Once again, Madelyne and I were looking for a rental home for our little family. (With Victor, who was born in 1947, we were three. Mark was born in '49.) Housing in Santa Rosa was tight and very little was available. In 1947, the city had a population of about 15,000, up from 12,000 before the war, which was why housing was so scarce. We placed an ad in *The Press Democrat* offering to exchange our apartment in Oakland for one in Santa Rosa. For more than a week, there was no response.

Then, one Saturday morning, I received a call from Margo Pierson. She said that she and her husband had a ranch home on their "estate" which they would exchange for our unit in Oakland. As soon as I hung up the telephone, we were on our way to Santa Rosa. Following her directions, with some difficulty, we finally found her "estate," a little hillside ranch in Rincon Valley at the end of Wallace Road, which turned off Brush Creek Road. Wallace Road was graveled and the last quarter mile to the ranch was dirt. Upon seeing the so-called home, our jaws dropped. It was an old, vacant ranch house, in grave disrepair, having been occupied by tenants who, to say the least, were not the best of housekeepers.

Madelyne could easily have said, "If you think I will stay in that shack, you are wrong." Instead, quite typical of her, she said, "Oh, we can clean it up, do some alterations. It will do." Had she objected, we probably would have returned to Oakland, and who knows what direction our lives would have taken. Madelyne was true to her word. She made the little house quite presentable. For the months we lived there, before buying a home in the Grace Tract in town, she and our year-old Victor would walk down the road to greet me every evening at 5 o'clock. Then, one day, as we sat on a bench in the back yard, I casually mentioned that I could see a snake in the grassy area nearby and that I thought it might be a rattler. This occasioned an immediate decision to find a house in town.

Meanwhile I had found an office. Again, rental space was limited. But I found one room, about 400 square feet on the fourth floor of the Rosenberg Building, located in downtown Santa Rosa, across from the county courthouse in the town square. With a rented desk and chair and a typewriter and a telephone, I was in business.

The permanent name I chose for my company was Sonoma Mortgage Corporation. We weren't a corporation, because at the time the company was owned by an individual. But "corporation" sounded impressive, and there were no legal objections. My first step was to go to *The Press Democrat* advertising department and arrange to have a large ad published with the phrase "4% for home loans" prominently displayed. I remember that Paul Johnson, the newspaper's long-time advertising manager, was skeptical of this newcomer. "That will be cash in advance," he told me.

No sooner was I settled in than the phone started ringing. Many of the inquiries were from people who could not qualify, but gradually the solid prospects increased, and soon I was generating two or three loans a week. For clerical help at the start, on a limited budget, I was able to hire Libby Roberts. At first, she was only able to work in the afternoon since her son, Gary, was a baby and she had to stay home in the mornings. This worked out well, as I would do all my work in the morning. She would come in at 1 p.m. and complete all the typing, correspondence and loan preparation. In the afternoon, I would go out to make contact with possible borrowers and do other necessary work in the field to arrange loan presentations to Northwestern Mutual.

In addition to finding borrowers for Northwestern Mutual, I was seeking opportunities as a loan appraiser. At the appraiser's course in San Francisco the year before, I had met Elmer Gascoigne. He had also attended the classes and had taken a job as head of the loan guarantee department of the Veteran's Administration in California. This department guaranteed qualified loans, promising to repay the lender if the borrower defaulted. I contacted Elmer and, with his influence, he made me a qualified appraiser for the VA.

The VA's loan guarantee could only be as high as 100 percent of the appraiser's report. In Santa Rosa, few VA-guaranteed loans were made. This was because two other appraisers appointed by the VA were officers of the local Santa Rosa Savings & Loan, and they were influenced in their valuations by the S&L's conservative lending practices. The numerous delinquencies of home loans in the 1930s, before World War II, had made lenders wary. Consequently, many of the VA appraisal reports made in Sonoma County were lower than the asking sales price. My appraisals, which I believed were conscientiously accurate, usually equaled the asking price. Suddenly, I was getting the majority of the requests for VA appraisals. My fee, set by the VA, was $20 for each appraisal. Mind you, at the time, homes of the average residential style were selling for between $6,000 and $12,000.

Money for mortgages was extremely limited. Many VA-guaranteed loans were granted by lending institutions as a patriotic gesture. Also available were Federal Housing Administration guarantees for loans. But many banks and savings and loan companies in the western part of the United States placed what loans they made on a conventional loan basis without VA or FHA guarantees, because rates were higher and terms were shorter.

On the East Coast, mutual savings banks predominated and were quite active, but state law usually limited their operations to their home state. During World War II, with restrictions on domestic construction, mutual savings banks often put excess funds in government bonds. These yielded, at the most, 1½ percent. After the war, states began altering their rules, allowing mutual savings banks to loan in contiguous states. Later, under pressure for better yields, mutual savings banks got approval to loan nationwide, but only with VA and FHA loans. This had a significant impact in the western states where there was a more dramatic shortage of funds. Excellent opportunities for mortgage bankers developed.

Within a year, SMC's volume of loans increased enough so that our office in the Rosenberg Building became too small. A former jewelry store at 220 Hinton Avenue became available. Hinton was a one-block street on the east side of the courthouse. Our new office was 20 feet by 50 feet, adjacent to the Topaz Room, Santa Rosa's fanciest dining establishment, two doors away from city hall, in the same block as the county jail.

The front of the building needed upgrading, so we added a green tile façade with pleated stainless steel trim and a prominent sign saying "LOANS!"

Libby was working full time now, and we hired one typist to assist her. We were not, as yet, a loan company that serviced loans. Once a loan was completed, it was transferred to Northwestern Mutual. It was a growing business. We contracted with Western Mortgage Co., the exclusive lender for Metropolitan Life, and with Hibernia Bank of San Francisco. They were accepting loans that Northwestern could not, paying me a 1 percent fee.

I got the idea that it would be profitable to start a small-loan company to make loans on automobiles and furniture. At a Chamber of Commerce meeting, I met John Cunningham, a handsome, well-dressed man about my age, which was then the early 30s. He had been an Army officer and was managing a small-loan company in Santa Rosa. After some consideration, I asked him if he would like to join me in starting a small-loan company. He agreed. There was room in our Hinton Avenue office for him, and we hired a clerk to assist him. Again, the timing was right. It took only a bit of newspaper advertising for personal loan applications to started flowing in. We supported the loans with a line of credit from Bank of America. For over a year we were very active in both real estate lending and small-loan lending. Things went well for the first year. The small-loan department had increased in volume, and we decided it was time to sell. Household Finance, a national small-loan company, bought the portfolio.

By then, real estate loans were expanding, and it was apparent that they were the future of SMC. John Cunningham became the vice president and Dorothe Hutchinson, our accountant, became the treasurer. My first employee, Libby Roberts, was secretary of the corporation. With some clerical help, the four of us carried forth the expansion of the company.

Mutual savings banks in the eastern cities could double or triple their income by selling their lower-yield government bonds and making government-insured real estate loans instead. They were very interested and willing to purchase mortgages we arranged. WWII veterans, many of them newly educated on the GI Bill, were buying homes with VA loans. And the post-war prosperity meant that others had incomes that qualified them for home loans. We were in an excellent position to take advantage of arranging loans for builders, as the demand increased. We would contact a builder interested in building a subdivision, offering mortgage assistance. We then needed to find a source for the final financing, generally for mortgages lasting 25 and 30 years. Local banks were certainly interested in making construction loans, but none had the capacity to maintain the volume of loans needed in this expanding economy.

In my student days at UC Berkeley, one of my most valuable courses was called "Money and Banking," taught by Professor John K. Langdon, who subsequently became president of the Federal Reserve Bank in Chicago.

A classmate, Raymond Lapin, and I had done research for Langdon as part of a class project, and we became friends. Raymond's aunt and uncle, Kitty and Ben Goldberg, had a home in the hills of Berkeley. They often invited us for brunch on Sundays, always a very enjoyable affair. The friendship grew and we maintained contact with one another while Ray served as an officer in the Army in the Philippines and I was in the Aleutian Islands.

After the war, Ray was employed by John Langdon and also took an advanced course in banking at Rutgers University. Among his classmates were officers of mutual savings banks. It was Ray who established my first connection with mutual savings banks and assisted me in other contacts with these banks. Mutual savings banks were eager to become active in our area, but they were apprehensive of associating with a small, new mortgage company. Their first choice was a well-established lending institution. It was Ray's influence that helped us in the early contacts with people he knew from Rutgers.

Ray then approached me with a request to become an owner and shareholder of Sonoma Mortgage. I considered it, but decided we were doing fine with our small group, so I refused. We remained on friendly terms and Ray started his own company in San Francisco, called Bankers Mortgage. He thrived and, much earlier than my own merger, merged his company with Transamerica Corporation. Ray and the president of Mortgage Bankers Association, aided by Senator Alan Cranston of California, started the government-owned Federal National Mortgage Association, known as Fannie Mae. Senator Cranston was a strong Democrat, as was Ray.

Ray became president of Fannie Mae and was highly respected for the immediate good reputation the government agency acquired. When Nixon became president in 1969, he asked Ray to resign and gave the position to a Republican. Ray always contended that he delayed his resignation to assure that all employees received proper benefits (i.e. medical and retirement). Because Ray delayed his resignation, Nixon actually fired him. The significance of being fired rather than resigning negatively affected Ray's reputation. Had he resigned, he would have received offers to become director of some large institutions. Instead, he simply resumed his position as a mortgage broker.

My first East Coast banking contact was American Irving Savings Bank in New York City. The loan officer, John Hammett, took a liking to me. He even visited us at our Santa Rosa home. He was willing to fund my account. When I completed a loan and sold it to American Irving, the borrowers still made their monthly payments to Sonoma Mortgage. The payment included principal, interest and property taxes. This involved setting up a loan servicing department. In the early 1950s, this was done manually, without computers and complex lending software that was still 30 years in the future. With Dorothe Hutchinson's considerable expertise, we set up our program.

After American Irving, more eastern savings banks came on board as another source of funds. I went back and forth to New York almost on a semi-monthly basis, even visiting other banks. For mutual savings bank officers, crossing the country was itself a very prestigious and popular opportunity. Of course, they had to inspect the properties prior to committing to purchase the loan when a house was finished. These commitments were generally for one year. With that commitment, we could take the deal to a commercial bank, usually the Bank of America, who in turn would offer the construction financing. The builder then commenced building his tract homes, generally completing them in five to six months.

Sonoma County was growing quickly. Developers like Hugh Codding, Charlie Cornish and Eugene Personett, James Blackwell and Gene Service were building large tracts on the edges of Santa Rosa. Codding, particularly, was bent on changing the face of the town. When his Montgomery Village development was annexed to Santa Rosa in 1955, the population of the city went from 17,000 to 31,000 in that single day.

Our operations spread through Sonoma County and into Marin, then to the East Bay and Sacramento. For the expansion, we acquired competent field loan solicitors. Our clerical personnel requirements grew so fast that we were again running out of space in our small office on Courthouse Square. We added space on the second floor of the building, but the quarters were still not adequate for the long haul.

In the late 1950s, I purchased three lots on the corner of 4th street and Proctor Drive in Santa Rosa. The entrance fronted on a well-established residential area. We needed an architect who would build something that suited the neighborhood and met our needs. I hired Germano Milono, a San Francisco architect. He designed a one-story building to fit easily on these three 60-by-120-foot lots. The floor plan had almost twice the space we

~ 61 ~

needed at that time.

The local Internal Revenue Service office, also needing new space, agreed to lease the remaining area. The city planning commission approved Milono's one-story design. The contract went to Wright Construction Company. Financing was through Wells Fargo Bank. Before construction began, the IRS announced that it would require much more space than originally thought. So, Gerry Milono said, "Well, the only way we can do it is to go to two floors."

We agreed, and Milono drew an acceptable plan for a two-story structure. Of course, it had to be re-submitted to the city planners. There was no problem getting the new plans approved. But the neighbors weren't as accepting. The steel frame of the building was installed in one day and when the people who lived in homes nearby saw the steel beams, two-stories high, they were in an uproar. I happened to be in New York at the time, but John Cunningham told me what was happening. He said, "If I were you, I don't think I would come into town for a while, until this thing cools down."

Apparently, as hard as it is to believe, the planning commission approved the new design without realizing that it called for two floors. We all did a lot of tall talking and, in time, we were able to find common ground with neighbors and the members of the planning commission, and the building progressed.

The following years were very active. We obtained servicing accounts with many of the mutual savings banks, including Bowery, East River, Harlem, Philadelphia Savings Society and Dry Dock. All of these agreements were reached with routine trips to New York and put together with the participation of our New York broker, Jack Eleford, and his assistant, Marilyn Brown.

(I should explain here that negotiating with builders always required both skill and hard work. An example is what happened several years later, when President Nixon removed the freeze on interest rates, causing them to fluctuate wildly. As the rates went up, builders wanted to re-negotiate to lower rates while the banks held firm at the higher yields. It was always a risky business.)

~ 62 ~

As Sonoma Mortgage grew, it became apparent that additional capitalization would be necessary in order to efficiently manage a good flow of mortgages. To make loans to builders and home-buyers, we needed to have a line of credit. We could then warehouse the loans until all documentation was completed for final delivery to the institution purchasing the loans.

Banks like Bank of America and Wells Fargo gave us lines of credit to handle these loans. They were insistent that, when a home loan was finally processed, there was an identified institution to buy the mortgage rather than the loan sitting in our portfolio until we found one. We thought that a better solution would be for us to have adequate capital to keep the loans in our own portfolio rather than selling them immediately.

My options, I decided, were to secure a partner, go public, or merge with some other mortgage institution. Some of our interim lending was with Wells Fargo Bank. James B. Keegan was the Santa Rosa manager and a very close friend. For some years our homes were adjacent to one another and our families were close. Billie, Jim's wife, was a good friend to my wife Madelyne, and Jim Keegan Jr. was a friend to Victor and Mark.

As it happened, officials in the home office of Wells Fargo were talking about the possibility of expanding into a more aggressive mortgage loan operation. Jim, who was highly respected by the bank, suggested to them that Sonoma Mortgage Corporation might be a likely candidate. After the usual negotiations, Wells Fargo's board of directors approved the acquisition. The terms included an exchange of Wells Fargo stock for the book value of all assets and a value of ½ -of-1 percent for the mortgages in the portfolio that we were servicing at the time, approximately $4 million.

That, plus the book value, equaled 5.5 million shares of stock. We became the largest stockholder of Wells Fargo Bank.

It was an enviable position to be in – until we were pre-empted by Warren Buffett of Berkshire Hathaway and Ambassador Walter Annenberg, both of whom made acquisitions larger than ours.

I, in turn, gave my principal officers, namely John Cunningham,

Dorothe Hutchinson, Libby Roberts and a few others, 20 percent of the Wells stock and we all became employees of Wells Fargo Bank. This was in 1963, 16 years after the start of SMC. One of our assets in Sonoma Mortgage was my investment in the Oakland Raiders, which I will explain in another chapter. Wells Fargo, being state chartered, was not allowed to own subsidiary companies. When the company acquired all our assets, ownership of a football team did not fit the bank regulators' criteria, so I bought back the 5 percent interest in the Raiders for $300,000. ❖❖❖

CHAPTER VII ~ WELLS FARGO

Sonoma Mortgage became the mortgage loan division of Wells Fargo. I became senior vice president. John Cunningham became a vice president, as did Dorothe Hutchison and Libby Roberts, who had the distinction of being the first women to hold that title at Wells Fargo. They had been vice presidents at Sonoma Mortgage and I saw no reason to pass them by. It is interesting to note that today women may well outnumber the men as vice presidents of the bank. John Cunningham became operations manager, Libby worked in processing and Dorothe was my administrative assistant. Less than two years later, John was with clients one evening in San Jose when he suddenly became ill and died. This, of course, profoundly shocked all of us but especially his wife, Jill, and their two daughters, Susan and Cathy.

Dorothe assumed John's position. When the bank chose to trans-fer from the Fourth Street office to larger facilities, she supervised and directed construction of a new building just north of Santa Rosa on Highway 101, which later would become offices for Sutter Health physicians plus a very popular café called Chloe's.

Meanwhile, though I had other interests that I will describe later, I was honored to be asked to be a member of the Wells Fargo Board of Directors. I served until I was 70 years old, which was the age of compulsory retirement for directors. If it had not been compulsory, I might have stayed longer since I found being on the board offered many new opportunities. Naturally, I attended the board meetings regularly, where I found there was a pleasant new tradition. At each director's seat, at each meeting, there was an envelope containing 10 crisp $100 bills. This was our remuneration for attendance. This remained a tradition throughout my time on the board.

Prior to joining the board, while I was still a senior vice president, President and chief executive officer Richard Cooley, in conjunction with the board, decided the bank needed a subsidiary Real Estate Investment Trust (REIT). At the time Wells Fargo acquired Sonoma Mortgage Corporation, Wells was a state charter bank. Subsequently it became a federal charter bank, which enabled it to have subsidiaries in its portfolio.

A member of the faculty at the Stanford Graduate School of Business was retained to assemble the REIT and make it functional. Because I was head of the mortgage loan department, I became the chairman of Wells Fargo REIT. But, realistically, I was a figurehead. John Holman was one of the more influential officers of the bank. And – to use the vernacular – he called the shots. Bank officers performed all the functions of organizing the structure, including the recruitment of personnel to run the operation.

A number of prominent, well-qualified individuals applied for the REIT president's job, including the vice president of a small bank in Los Angeles. His name was Carl Reichardt. Although the committee debated the merits of three other candidates, it was Holman who said, flatly, "We will offer the position to Carl Reichardt." Carl accepted. In the negotiation for salary, he asked for and received 10 percent of the REIT stock. Wells Fargo chairman Ernie Arbuckle, former dean of the Stanford Graduate School of Business, and president Richard Cooley, were so impressed with Reichardt over time that they transferred him from president of the REIT to senior vice president of the bank. Within a short time he became Wells Fargo's president.

During Reichardt's presidency, some of his junior officers distinguished themselves in the financial world. Robert Joss became chief executive officer of one the largest banks in Australia. Later, he was Dean of the Graduate School of Business at Stanford. John Grundhofer became president and chairman of U.S. Bancorp. Carl Reichardt's administrative ability contributed to the overall success of the bank. Besides his leadership of Wells Fargo, he served on the boards of PG&E, The Irvine Company of Newport Beach, ConAgra Foods (a large food corporation in Omaha, Nebraska), and Ford Motor Company (where he became vice chairman in charge of finance).

The monthly meetings of the 16 members of the Wells Fargo board I enjoyed for years were always well planned, with a familiar routine of officers' reports. I found this very different from the several boards of smaller companies I served on, where there was always considerable discussion (and argument) among the members. If there were arguments at Wells Fargo, they took place among the executives, before they came to the board. This made the job much easier. I served on the compensation committee, which annually reviewed the salaries of the senior officers, including the president and chairman. Robert Joss was an advisor to the committee and provided information about comparable salaries from other companies.

One meeting of the board stands out in my memory as one of the most interesting experiences in my tenure. In the 1970s, the bank became more aggressive in its international operations. Vice President Carlos Rodriguez-Pastor headed that department. Carlos's experience and training made him an outstanding manager.

At the time, South American bankers were increasingly concerned about the economies of their major countries such as Argentina, Chile, Peru and Brazil. Inflation was rampant, as high as 150 percent in Argentina. Unemployment was high and the political environment appeared unstable. Members of the Wells board voiced concern, particularly with the bank's growing volume of activity. At the meeting it was arranged that Carl Reichardt and I would visit the major cities in South America and judge for ourselves what the future of our involvement should be.

On September 5, 1979, Carl and I, Carlos Rodriguez-Pastor, and the second in command of the South American division, Fernando Holman, departed from San Francisco for a 12-day tour. Prior to departure, Carl and I were given three binders of information, one for each of the cities we were to visit. These were approximately 100 pages each. They set forth a schedule of times for meetings, background information about the officials we would meet with and a complete history of the banks involved in that country.

Here is an example of a routine day. This happens to be the

first day in Lima, Peru.

September 5th
- 6 p.m. Departure, Braniff
- 6:15 a.m. Arrive in Lima
- 10 a.m. First call to Minister of Economy and Finance of the Republic of Peru
- 10:30 a.m. Call on Minister of the Central Bank
- 12:00 p.m. Call on General Pedro Richter, Prime Minister
- 1:15 p.m. Luncheon hosted by Banco Credito Del Peru, with nine chairmen or presidents of the major banks and investment houses
- 4:30 p.m. Visit to Gold Museum
- 7:00 p.m. Cocktails hosted by Manuel Allov, chairman of Faucett Airlines
- 9:00 p.m. Dinner hosted by Banco de la Nacíon, with 12 chairmen or presidents of major companies

All three countries' schedules were similar with the exception of Sunday, when I prevailed upon Carl to join me in watching the polo matches at Te Palermo Polo Fields in Santiago, Chile. Polo was a sport that was to become a dominant part of my life in the years to come.

One memorable meeting was with General Augusto Pinochet, president of Chile and commander-in-chief of the army. As I recall, we met at a truly elaborate building called Villa Vecencio. Four military officers greeted us and escorted us into the main offices of President Pinochet. He was quite a dashing military figure in the imposing uniform of a general. As we entered his stately hall, we were surprised to see television cameras awaiting our entrance. What was to have been a courtesy call developed into a well-publicized event, broadcast through all the television networks in Chile.

We were unwitting players in a publicity maneuver – two American bankers paying a visit of solicitation to Chile's president. Since Pinochet's ironclad dictatorship was very controversial, the video of our visit became something of a political issue. I suppose you could say that this was my 15 minutes of (unwanted) fame in Chile.

As I previously noted, the compulsory retirement age for Wells Fargo Bank board members was 70. So, in 1990, I became an honorary member of the board. I was still allowed to meet with the board in an emeritus, non-voting status. Because of the large number of shares that the Triones owned (we were the largest stock-holding family), I continued to keep close track of the actions of the board.

The progress of the bank was largely successful through the years. The mergers of the Norwest Corporation and Wells Fargo did much to make it one of the largest mortgage banks in the country. Richard (Dick) Kovacevich became chairman and proved an able administrator. The dividends went as high as $1.20 per share, which provided a substantial flow of income to our family – at least until the crash of 2008, when dividends were reduced to 20 cents per share, a dramatic reduction which we shared with stockholders around the country.

Whenever I saw Dick Kovacevich at some social function, I would raise my hand suggesting he increase the dividends. One day in 2009, he put a stop to that. "What are you complaining about?" he said. "The amount we give you each year is more than you have invested in the bank."

He was right. So I shut up. ❖❖❖

PART TWO

*Thus far, you've heard the story of my life
in the order in which it happened.
These early chapters, as you have seen,
are pretty much chronological. My family.
My early years. My military service. My exploration
of the business world, which proved interesting
and rewarding. But there's much more to tell.
There have been many adventures on the road
I have been blessed to travel.*

*In the second part of this memoir,
I will share them with you, in no particular order.
Call them what you will – adventures, enterprises,
opportunities. Each one is a story of its own –
an episode in my long life, distinct chapters
in the story of this "baker boy."*

CHAPTER VIII ~ TIMBERRRRR!

The familiar cry that is the title of this chapter is the timber faller's warning that a big tree, destined for the mill, is about to come down. It was a familiar sound in the Humboldt County of my youth and, in fact, all along the coastal regions of Northern California. I cannot recall ever hollering "timberrr!" but I gained a great respect for those who do. My involvement in this important 20th century industry did not include falling trees but rather some interesting investments in companies that were involved in the process, from axe to lumber yard.

One morning in July 1963, I was in my office at Sonoma Mortgage Corporation when my secretary, Phyllis McCann, told me Mr. James Laier wanted to see me. I had met Jim briefly at the opening night's festivities of the Sonoma County Trail Blazers Trek in early June but did not know him well. I had no idea what he wanted to see me about, but I immediately stepped out, greeted him and invited him in. He had come to tell me that his partner in Molalla Forest Products, Norman Delaittre, was ready to retire. Jim wanted to know if I was interested in purchasing Delaittre's share of this million-dollar investment.

I was intrigued by the idea. But I knew I did not have the surplus funds available. Sonoma Mortgage's need for working capital required most of our assets. The local banks that warehoused our loans, pending preparation of documents to be submitted to the final lender that would buy them, were always seeking more collateral security for loaning us interim funds. We needed cash on hand because of the time involved between paying off the construction loan and being reimbursed by the ultimate lenders. These were usually eastern savings banks that purchased the loans.

I explained the situation but I also told Jim that I was very interested in his proposition. He proposed a minimal down payment with the balance to come from my share of future earnings in the company. After a few days of consideration, I

~ 72 ~

agreed, and the transaction was completed. I was now part owner of a company with a lumber mill, 33,000 acres of timberland and an excellent cash flow.

Since the first settlers arrived on the Pacific Coast, the availability of timber had made lumber the construction product of choice. Redwood timber, though relatively soft in texture, has excellent preserving strength. Its abundance and accessibility in Humboldt and Mendocino counties provided a ready resource for flourishing mills. In the first towns, even the sidewalks were made of 2 x 12 redwood planks.

Beginning in 1850, fortunes were made in redwood. The "Timber Rush" to the North Coast of California, some say, built San Francisco twice, once after the Gold Rush and again after the 1906 earthquake. The availability of redwood was one of the factors in Santa Rosa's post-war building boom. It played a part in my decision to go into the mortgage business in Santa Rosa after World War II.

For several generations, family names like Hammond, Carson, Murphy and Simpson were associated with lumber and, most important, with the prosperity of the coastal areas. A fine example of the kind of lifestyle redwood afforded these entrepreneurs can be seen in the Carson House overlooking Humboldt Bay in Eureka. This three-story "gingerbread" house, which draws tourists to the Eureka waterfront, is a classic example of American Queen Anne architecture and a monument to the redwood lumber industry. The most-photographed house in California, it was constructed in 1884 by pioneer lumberman William Carson, who imported craftsmen from Europe for the intricate work. It was owned by the Carson family until 1950 when it became the home of the Ingomar Club, a social club for prominent Humboldt businessmen – a kind of North Coast answer to San Francisco's Pacific-Union Club.

Through the decades, the abundance of virgin redwood was so great that no one voiced concern that these magnificent old-growth trees, which took centuries to grow, could disappear. Lumber companies had all they felt they needed. Redwood acreage was readily available for purchase. I recall my father saying in

1930 that he could have acquired a section of virgin redwood just for the taxes. But, as the pace of depletion increased, there was concern that the old-growth trees might be eliminated. Lumber companies began reforestation projects, since redwood grows quickly. And, in 1918, an organization called the Save the Redwoods League was formed in San Francisco to promote conservation of the redwood forests.

Over time, vast areas of timberland became parkland, both state and national, protected forever from the faller's axe and saw. Redwoods preservation advocates now complain that only 5 percent of the existing timberland is free from commercial exploitation. However, their 5 percent amounts to quite enough acreage, others say, considering the cost of management.

Meantime, the cost of virgin redwood has skyrocketed in value. As an example, our family's Flatridge Ranch – part of the Kelly tract in northwestern Sonoma County – had a large redwood near a stream that, without erosion control, fell on its own. It was 92 inches in diameter at its base. When commercial tree-cutting methods are used to fell a tree, loggers work to avoid what they call "whiplash," which results in splintering and can render much of the tree useless for lumber. In the instance of the tree in the Kelly tract, naturally, no precautions were taken. Yet the remainder of the tree and its broken pieces yielded more than $10,000 cash.

The value of the timber industry varied through the years with the cyclical fluctuations of the economy. The Great Depression of the 1930s brought an abrupt end to the demand for timber. This caused severe hardships on employees as well as employers in the industry. One example was the Pacific Lumber Co. in Humboldt, owned by the Murphy family of San Francisco. The company owned the mill town of Scotia on the Eel River – all the houses leased to employees, the general store, the gasoline station, the hotel, the bank, the theater, the hospital and even the slaughterhouse where company livestock was processed. In Depression years, as I have discussed in an earlier chapter, the company issued Scotia scrip, redeemable at company businesses. It was an aid to the townspeople, both working and unemployed.

Even stores in nearby towns would accept the scrip whenever reasonable.

In times of building booms, timber prices rise, and it was in a boom time, early in the 1950s, that Laier and Delaittre, both former employees of Pope & Talbot lumber company in Oregon, developed a lumber mill near Cloverdale. They called it Molalla Forest Products Co. The name came from the name of a town in Oregon. They chose Cloverdale as the mill site because, despite the increased building, it was still a time when timberlands could be purchased from ranchers at very nominal prices. Ranchland in Sonoma County containing reasonable amounts of timber was selling at prices as low as $25 an acre. In some instances, lumbermen would purchase the land, harvest the timber and sell the residual ranch on the open market.

Meanwhile, Paul and Lucile Kelly, who had been in the timber business in Prineville, Oregon, had become interested in the timber in northwestern Sonoma County . Much of it was inaccessible. New roads, they reasoned, could create markets for isolated stands of timber. Consequently, they developed the Kelly Road, which began just south of Cloverdale, contiguous to the Molalla Mill, and extended some 21 miles westward, close to the small town of Annapolis.

Lumbermen would come to consider this project a stroke of genius. On the private road, trucks could haul loads considerably heavier than what was allowed on public highways. And insurance was considerably less, thus decreasing the cost of trucking. For use of the Kelly Road, truckers were charged $3 per thousand running-feet of timber. When Paul Kelly died – as the road was still under construction – his wife Lucile took over the company, completed the road, operated it and made a fortune.

In turn, ranch owners benefited from the road and lumber companies acquired logs at a very competitive price. At the time I joined Jim Laier, Molalla was actively purchasing most of the logs coming off the Kelly Road. Jim, on occasion, would mention that we should acquire the road for future benefits.

By coincidence, Mrs. Kelly lived next door to us on Montecito

Avenue in Santa Rosa. She had purchased from Madelyne and me the single-family lot contiguous to our home and built a home there. For some reason, Jim was reluctant to negotiate with her, but, since we were neighbors, I often stopped by, usually in the late afternoon or early evening. We both would enjoy a martini and she would smoke a cigarette.

At first approach, she was sentimentally opposed to selling the Kelly Road because she thought of it as something of a tribute to the business acumen of her late husband. But, eventually, she agreed to a sale and a price of $200,000. The purchase included portions of land along the road that the Kellys had acquired in the original purchase. There was one section of 1,150 acres, which she called "Kelly Lodge." She was unable to sell it because Ed Norton, owner of the adjoining Flatridge Ranch, had an option to purchase the land at $8 an acre should she elect to sell. It was my son Mark who negotiated with Norton and bought his option for $20,000.

We then offered Mrs. Kelly $100 an acre for the 1,150 acres of Kelly Lodge land. At first she refused, again for sentimental reasons involving Paul. He had particularly enjoyed the site, with its creek, forest and isolation from the busy world of Highway 101. But I also believe that $100 an acre just didn't sound like much to her. The next offer we made was for $115,000. This time she agreed.

Meanwhile, Molalla acquired the Mad River Lumber Company in Humboldt, east of Arcata, on the Mad River. Jim was of the opinion that Weyerhaeuser, the large lumber firm from Washington and Oregon, might sell its interests in Northern California. In his opinion, the California property did not fit that company's overall operations. Weyerhaeuser's investment in California included 36,000 acres of land, vast stands of marketable timber, a complete logging operation, a particleboard plant, and a large lumber mill, which was located just north of Arcata on Highway 101.

We made some preliminary inquiries, and, in response, Jim received a phone call from Bill Lowery, a Weyerhaeuser executive, indicating that the company might consider the sale. He suggested a date when we could meet in their executive offices in Tacoma, Washington, and Jim agreed but subsequently realized that he and Gunther Hardt were booked on a hunting expedition in Central Africa at that time. Rather than change the date, he suggested that Dick Smith, our controller, and I go north and meet with the Weyerhaeuser people.

I was very apprehensive about the meetings, as I was only too aware of my limited knowledge of the industry. But Jim said, "Just go up and see what they have to say." So I agreed, and Smith and I flew up for the meeting in Tacoma. After a casual discussion over coffee, we were escorted into the directors' room, where no less than 10 executives and lawyers were waiting. We were seated in the center and given an illustrated brochure explaining the proposed sale. As we went through the detailed pages, I asked some questions that I hoped would indicate knowledge of the operation. Finally, I said, "This looks very interesting but my question is: How much and when?" As I recall, Lowery replied that the price was $12 million, all in cash. I assured them I thought it was worth looking into, but asked for time to discuss it with our financing sources and accounting firm.

It was obvious to me that the whole proposal was well beyond our financial means. I was simply stalling until Jim returned and we could discuss the matter. We got together when he returned from Africa and it didn't take us long to figure out that the only way was to involve one or two other interested parties.

Our first contact was with Sierra Pacific, a company owned by Red Emmerson and John Crook. John was not interested, but Red was. Eventually, he agreed to join us. Simpson Lumber Co. in Tacoma was interested, so negotiations began.

The first step was for the three principals to decide how the assets should be distributed. Simpson wanted the 36,000 acres of land plus the logging operation. In a meeting with Weyerhaueser about dividing the assets, we came to the point where we were $300,000 apart. And neither party would budge.

That's when the Weyerhaeuser chairman excused himself

and went to the men's room. By coincidence, I went too. As we were standing there, urinal-to-urinal, I suggested we might split the difference. "Oh, hell," he said, "It's five o'clock and I need a drink." And the transaction was settled.

The Elk River stand of 5,000 acres of redwoods located south of Eureka was part of the package. It had been logged in the 1890s and the second growth had become mature enough for logging. In addition, residual logs on the ground, left when the prime timber was cut in the 1890s, were still in marketable condition when we purchased the land. They sold as first growth along with selected logging of the second growth, an indication of redwood's preservative nature.

After the selected logging was completed, Red Emmerson, Laier and I owned the land. About 1983, Emerson and Laier placed their portion in their foundation and offered me a price of $400,000 for my portion, which I accepted. Subsequently, the National Park Service purchased the land from Jim and Red for more than $10 million. My selling price was miniscule compared to the government offer. But then as now, a deal is a deal.

The Masonite Company was a large producer of a building material known internationally as, simply, Masonite. The main facility was in Laurel, Mississippi. The headquarters were in Chicago. As the company grew in California, Masonite built a particleboard plant in Ukiah. They also acquired large timberlands and a logging operation. The acquisition of our Molalla Forest Products Co. was a logical step for them. Typical of my style of business, being conservative and mindful of my family's losses in the Great Depression, I was ready to sell Molalla Forest Products in exchange for Masonite stock. And so was Jim.

With the merger of Molalla into Masonite, there was a seat for one of us on the board of directors. Jim was not interested, but I accepted and enjoyed my tenure. The directors met on a quarterly basis, generally at their Chicago headquarters. On occasion, we would meet at one of the major plants – Laurel, Mississippi; Columbus, Ohio; or Ukiah, California.

These meetings were interesting and enjoyable. The local and corporate staff would spend the mornings giving the board a financial report. Then they would provide a pleasant day, viewing operations.

One issue that arose involved South Africa. At that time – the 1970s – corporations that did business with South Africa were criticized for their involvement with apartheid. Some were even threatened with boycotts. Masonite executives, particularly Chairman John Coates and President Sam Greeley, were certain the plant in South Africa dealt fairly with employees, regardless of color. Chairman Coates felt the operation was unbiased and that it operated on an acceptable social level. But, because the issue was so intense, he invited board members to visit the plant and see for ourselves.

Madelyne and I, with another couple, accepted the invitation and traveled together to Cape Town, a very pleasant city on the Atlantic coast. Then we traveled 1,000 miles by overnight train to Johannesburg. We found the country fascinating and Johannesburg an attractive, cosmopolitan city. There, the three-tier racial system – black, brown and white – was very apparent. Our visit was brief but, as we went to hotels, restaurants and on city tours, all appeared to us to be harmonious. We were hosted and treated royally by the local company officers.

As far was we could tell, the three-tier system in the Masonite plant worked well. The company saw to it that workers in each tier had their own grievance committee. Many employees from local tribes worked bringing logs from the forests for the final processing into chips for particleboard.

Overall, we were satisfied with the operation and so advised the officers and board members in Chicago.

On the way back, we chose to go south to Durban, located on the Indian Ocean. There we had a chance to watch a polo match. Polo is enjoyed in many parts of South Africa where there are excellent horses of a somewhat different type from the thoroughbreds used in other parts of the polo world. In Durban we found that the influences of the countries surrounding the Indian Ocean were prevalent and created a different culture from the other cities we had seen.

Our return trip took us back to Cape Town. To spice up the trip even more, we returned to San Francisco via Brazil, spending several days in Rio de Janeiro. It was a very memorable trip.

In 1977, the board received information that a company from Chicago was about to make an unfriendly bid to acquire control of Masonite. This company knew that the vast acreage of land that Masonite owned was substantially higher in value than reported in the financial statements. Masonite officers called an emergency board meeting where directors decided that, in order to prevent this takeover bid, they would sell Masonite to a company that was more compatible.

They concluded that National Gypsum was the best suitor. I was the only member who voted against the proposal. My reasoning was that the board members of the unfriendly acquiring company could still work harmoniously with the Masonite management. But the board was anxious to assure the stockholders of National Gypsum there were no objections to the sale. So, in the interests of my relationship with the members of the board, I changed my vote. The board was then dissolved and National Gypsum operated the company until Masonite was sold off as a separate entity. The National Gypsum Company filed for bankruptcy in 2009.

What follows is a summary of my partnership with Jim Laier from my purchase of the Delaittre interest in 1963. That same year we acquired Blue Lake Lumber Company in Humboldt County from Robin Ackley. In 1965 we bought Weyerhaeuser Corporation's interest in Humboldt, Del Norte and Mendocino counties including 36,000 acres of timberland, a particleboard plant, a plywood plant and all the company's logging equipment in Humboldt. In 1968 we purchased the Kelly Road in Sonoma County, and in '69 we bought an Elk River stand of timber from the Chevey Company of Oregon. In addition we partnered with Red Emmerson in the Chainey Tract at Elk River. Emmerson owned 58 percent and Jim and I owned 42 percent. In 1970 Jim and I sold all of our Mollala stock to Masonite Corporation. ❖❖❖

CHAPTER IX ~ WIN SOME, LOSE SOME

Savings and loan franchises were strictly regulated and very hard to come by in the 1950s. It was a testament to developer Hugh Codding's aggressive nature that he managed, somehow, to get three S&L franchises – Mendo-Lake in Ukiah, Six Rivers in Eureka and Montgomery Village Savings & Loan in Santa Rosa. Montgomery Village S&L was only the second S&L in Santa Rosa and was regarded as something of an upstart alongside the well-established Santa Rosa Savings & Loan, run by J. Ralph Stone.

In 1956, Codding hit a bad patch of luck and teetered on the brink of bankruptcy. He was forced to sell some assets, including the S&L, which another Santa Rosa entrepreneur, Theron "Roy" Hedgpeth, took in lieu of money owed him. One day, in conversation with Roy, I told him that if he ever decided to get out of the S&L business I would be interested. Hedgpeth, who was considerably older and had already made a modest fortune, was not on a business expansion path. He took my offer seriously and in 1958 I bought the Montgomery Village S&L for about $91,000.

I invited several other investors to join me on the board of directors, including another good friend, attorney Charles DeMeo, who would surprise the town by leaving some $17 million to the Sonoma County Community Foundation for the benefit of young people and single mothers; Dan Bowerman, general manager of *The Press Democrat*; Fred Pedersen whose family furniture store was the oldest continuing business in Santa Rosa, dating to 1892; Leo Lamoreaux, owner of a soft drink distribution franchise; and Del Bevan, who owned a moving and storage company. We changed the name to Summit Savings and Loan.

California's post-war development spurred the S&L industry in the 1960s and '70s. There was substantial growth and Summit grew rapidly until the late 1960s when we merged with Imperial Corporation of America, the parent company of Imperial Savings Association. I sat on the board of Imperial for several years before selling my stock for a reasonable profit sometime around 1980.

Heeding the lessons of my father's 1929 experience was, as it turned out, a smart move since the federal deregulation acts of 1982, which lifted the strict rules that had governed S&Ls, led to a flood of abuses – S&Ls acting as developers, making questionable, too often illegal investments. Fortunately, my venture into the savings and loan business proved very successful, just as my son Victor's Luther Burbank Savings bank has been for him. I will, however, purposely avoid bragging about my boys and their achievements, hoping they will write their own memoirs one day.

I think this is a good place to talk about making money. I tell these stories, about buying low and selling high, as if there has been nothing but success in my financial life. I know that I am often accused of having "a Midas touch," which is flattering, but I tend to think of myself as a very lucky guy. Not always, however. Let me tell you about Burbank Development Company, a venture I do not for a moment regret because of its benefit to Santa Rosa. But I will readily admit that it was not an illustration of any so-called "Midas touch."

In the late 1950s, the federal Housing and Urban Development agency, known as HUD, offered cities funding to restore downtown areas that had been neglected in the war years and threatened by the new wave of suburban shopping centers (It was still too early to use the word "malls."). Known as Urban Renewal, this program allowed the government to purchase land in blighted areas, clear it and resell it for commercial use. In Santa Rosa the area south of the courthouse, including the former Chinatown, was old and, in some cases, neglected. This was the area the city fathers designated when they applied for and received Urban Renewal funds.

In December of 1963, five of us businessmen, anxious to see the downtown area survive as a center of commerce, formed the Burbank Development Company to buy these Urban Renewal properties. Partnering with me in this venture were my good friends Ralph Stone and Jim Keegan, along with Dan Bowerman; Ken Brown, owner of Corrick's, a stationary, office supply and gift store which had been on Fourth Street since 1916; and Medico Drug

Company's Angelo Franchetti. There were 40 limited partners in the company, each of whom invested $1,000, prompting Hugh Codding, whose Coddingtown regional shopping center north of town was busily attempting to lure downtown merchants at the time, to nickname us "Ali Baba and the Forty Thieves."

We had three major plans for the whole downtown complex, including one with a new civic center built over the square where the courthouse stood or another with a major hotel and major department store. The success of any of the plans was highly speculative. Potential buyers were very cautious. No one would jump first. For example, we were able to sell the corner of Third and Santa Rosa Avenue to Bank of America only after we agreed to buy its Fourth Street office, which was where Corrick's is today. It was pretty much the same for the other buildings. The General Services Administration would commit to construction of the Federal Building at Sonoma Avenue and E streets only after we purchased several parcels of excess government property in South San Francisco.

The result of all this deal making – which cost Ralph and me another million apiece to keep afloat – was three banks, a department store (a new home for the old White House at Third and E, which is now long gone), and the Imperial Savings & Loan offices on Santa Rosa Avenue.

The development of the Urban Renewal core eventually precipitated the construction of Eureka Federal's building at 50 Old Courthouse Square plus both the federal and state office buildings, The Redwoods office building at Sonoma Avenue and E Street and The Fountains on D Street, which is still my office and the offices of my sons Victor and Mark. So you'd have to say it was a great success as an upgrade of the downtown area. I have always felt that the company made a significant contribution to the identity of the downtown. But it didn't make money. It was definitely a non-profit venture. It wasn't intended to be, but that's the way it turned out. When the company disbanded in 1973, the "Ali Babas" and their gang received just 27 percent of their investment.

Now, in case you still believe that I have had nothing but success, I will recount the circumstances of my first financial disaster. It was sometime in the mid-1930s. I was working as a delivery boy for my father's Fortuna Bakery, a job that included, during an exciting week in the summer, deliveries to the Fortuna Rodeo. This was THE big event of the Humboldt County summer, and the concessions sold a lot of my father's hot dog and hamburger buns, as well as sweet rolls.

Hard on the heels of the rodeo came the Humboldt County Fair in Ferndale, where a Eureka café owner called Hamburger Charlie had the concession to sell hamburgers and hot dogs. Being young and full of bright ideas, I talked the rodeo concessionaire, whose name I cannot recall, into partnering with me to bid on the Fair's hamburger and hot dog concession.

The deal was if I got the bid, we would split the proceeds. I think he agreed because he didn't think I had a chance in the world of unseating Hamburger Charlie. But I bid. And I got it. It was all set up and looking good for my bold venture until opening day, when it started to rain and kept raining. And as if that wasn't enough, the guy we hired to make the hamburgers got drunk.

But what I remember most vividly about that summer was the telephone call I got from Dr. Cecil Jo Hindley, the president of the Fair's board of directors and an important man in the county. I think the committee members who awarded the bid to me felt they were giving a young man a chance. But I don't think Dr. Hindley saw it that way. He read me the riot act for daring to under-bid Hamburger Charlie who, he told me, was a bona fide legend at the Ferndale Fair. I had been, he said, disrespectful of tradition. I think he believed I was a "front" for the rodeo concessionaire. I didn't get a chance to explain that it really was my idea.

It wasn't all that great an idea, as it turned out. That summer was the beginning and end of my concessionaire career. I might have made $100. But I doubt it. I was 15 years old. ❖❖❖

CHAPTER X ~ EMPIRE COLLEGE

It all began with an empty building and a banker friend who thought I was joking. The distinctive four-story building in downtown Santa Rosa was on Exchange Avenue, a one-block street west of Courthouse Square. It had been the site of a financial institution since before the 1906 earthquake. Originally Santa Rosa Bank, it became the offices of Bank of Italy, which became Bank of America. For more than half a century, a bank occupied the ground floor while lawyers and accountants did business from the offices above.

Then, in 1961, Joe Lombardi, Bank of America's branch manager in Santa Rosa, determined that the bank needed more space and moved to new offices on Fourth Street (where Corrick's is at this writing), leaving the ground floor vacant. Several years passed and the number of upstairs tenants dwindled and disappeared.

One day, as Joe and I were talking, the discussion came around to the vacant building. The asking price, Joe told me, was about $365,000.

I said, "Joe, I'll offer you $100,000 provided you give me a $90,000 loan." He looked at me with genuine disgust. About a week later, he called.

"Were you serious about the offer on the building?" he asked.

I promptly said, "Yes," although I really had not given it another thought. But I went on to say that Bank of America would have to remove the restriction that the ground floor could not be leased to another lending institution.

His response was, "Oh, they would never agree to that." A week later he called again. "Okay," he said. "The restriction will be released."

So there I was – the owner of an obsolete building, with a lot of deferred maintenance, very close to becoming a genuine eyesore. I called my architect friend, Germano Milono, who designed our home and commercial buildings. I told him what I'd done and what I had on my hands. He was ready with suggestions.

Under Gerry's guidance, we repainted the exterior, redesigned the classic arches at the entrance, gilded the dome with sparkling gold leaf and repaired the clock to make it function again, a gesture that was well-received by the community. One more thing. We decided it could no longer be called the Bank of America Building. We needed a new name.

When it came to naming things, Madelyne was the one for the job. She was always quick and clever to come up with excellent names for our subdivisions and buildings. In this case, she came up with "Empire Building," derived from "Redwood Empire," the regional designation for the counties north of San Francisco Bay. So, Empire Building it was. And still is, I might add.

I leased the ground floor to First National Bank, but there was no activity in the vacant offices on the upper floors. Then, one day I was talking with Mary Thurman, who had a small employment agency specializing in clerical help. I was trying to convince her to lease office space in the building when I heard myself saying, impetuously, "Mary, the town needs a business school. Why don't you start one, and I'll give you the office space in the building." And then, having gone that far, I went farther. "If you need financing," I said, "I'll provide it. How much do you think you'll need?"

"Oh, I'm sure $5,000 will be adequate," she said. Little did I know that this was but a fragment of the financial requirement for the college in the years to come. As it came together, we needed a name, and there it was, on the building. It was only logical that we would call this new educational adventure "Empire College School of Business."

With the thriftiness that she had acquired managing her own business, Mary foraged for desks and chairs enough to furnish one classroom. With a supply of new and used typewriters, she was ready for the first 10 students. And then for 20. By the end of the first year, there were 50. Empire College was pronounced a success.

When Mary advised me, three years later, that she and her husband were moving to Portugal, I turned to colleague Dorothe Hutchinson, Sonoma Mortgage's treasurer, to run our growing business school. I can't say enough about Dorothe's part in the success of Empire College. As president as well as chair of the board of directors for almost 20 years, she played a significant role in the college's success. Since her death in 2002, I've said often that we should have called it Hutchinson College.

In 1973, Empire College added a School of Law, which, I think, surprised a Santa Rosa community that wondered if we could compete with the fine law schools in the Bay Area. But, from its inception, the law school has been a success story. We have been privileged to have excellent faculty and administration support from the legal community.

An active board of directors has been vital to the success of the school program. The college's advising attorney, John McDonald, has been a board member since its inception. Original directors were Charles DeMeo, Evert Person, Carroll Mjelde, Alan Milner and John McDonald, as well as Dorothe. The current board includes my son Victor, Stephen Hansel, Allen Gummer, Judy Coffey, Brad Bollinger, Barry Graham and the "originals," McDonald and Milner. Roy Hurd serves as chairman of the board and chief executive officer, and I am chairman of the executive committee.

In the 1960s, the 1910 courthouse in the square had been deemed unsafe and taken down, making the Empire Building the historic survivor in the center of the town. By that time, the combined educational facilities occupied almost all of the offices in the fine old building. That challenge had been met. The growing number of students and faculty – many of whom were retired teachers – brought complaints about lack of parking. Downtown merchants, who wanted shoppers in the parking spaces, not students rushing to and from classes, were increasingly critical. We decided it was time to find a new campus.

In 1965, developer Hugh Codding had built a sprawling building on Cleveland Avenue west of the freeway for State Farm Insurance Company. When State Farm moved its regional headquarters to Rohnert Park, the building was sold to a doctors' partnership and Dorothe, with my consent, arranged for Empire College to lease a sizeable portion of the building. It was an ideal

~ 87 ~

location, with plenty of parking.

After several years, the doctors' partnership had to sell the former State Farm Building with its vast lot and commercial zoning. The sale came at a financially fortuitous time. We had just sold a portion of the acreage near Geyser Peak Winery, which we had purchased several years earlier. In lieu of making an active capital outlay, we could transfer the funds from the vineyard sale to the acquisition of the acreage adjoining the old State Farm building with no tax payment required.

We retained the services of architect Eric Glass to design a new building on the site, incorporating a large parking lot sufficient for our present and future needs. Located on Highway 101 in north Santa Rosa, we now had an attractive building, which by its very presence enhanced the public's knowledge of the school. The County of Sonoma was seeking rental space for two municipal courtrooms and we were also able to incorporate these into the design of our building. This provided funds needed to service the debt. Also, the on-site courtrooms offered the college's law students direct experiences in how a court of law functions.

From its inception in the old Bank of America Building, Empire College, now more than 50 years old, has sustained remarkable growth. Again, I attribute much of its success to Dorothe Hutchinson and to the current president and CEO, Roy Hurd, and his wife, Sherie, who serves as the school's executive vice president. Their knowledge and experience has made it one of the most outstanding private business colleges in the nation.

The School of Business offers degrees and certification in accounting, information technology, legal assisting and medical technology as well as office administration. Employment rate for business graduates is in the 80 percent range. The School of Law boasts that its graduates regularly achieve one of the highest State Bar examination pass rates among California's accredited private law schools. The total cumulative pass rate average for the law school's 40-plus years of existence is 76 percent.

The faculty includes many outstanding local lawyers and judges, and its graduates make up about 25 percent of the Sonoma County

Bar and have contributed members of the judiciary in several Northern California counties.

In 2011, the Hurds organized a 50-year celebration that was attended by many community executives. John Stumpf, chairman and CEO of Wells Fargo Bank, was the featured speaker, reflecting the prominence the school has achieved in the Bay Area. Asked to speak about the school's history, I could only suggest that an acorn grows into an oak tree.

And grow it has. In 2012, Empire College had about 1,000 students enrolled and had more than 10,000 graduates over its 51-year history. That same year the school was honored to become the only private for-profit college to be named on the President's Higher Education Community Service Honor Roll, a national award recognizing colleges and universities that inspire lifelong civic engagement among their students. It is one of 110 honor roll schools named "with distinction," and one of only 18 colleges in California so designated.

When a local magazine writer asked me, in 2012, to name my proudest philanthropic achievement, I answered "Empire College," which, I think, surprised him. Despite the fact that it is a business venture, not philanthropy, I rank it as an important contribution, I told him, because it has afforded so many young people a higher level of income, making a better life for them and, consequently, for the whole community. ❖❖❖

CHAPTER XI ~ THE FRUIT OF THE VINE

My family's winery, on the site of a 105-year-old Italian winery built of the distinctive stone that is part of Sonoma County's historic landscape, is a source of great pride for me. My interest in wine like my taste for truffles is, I'm sure, inherited. There was always wine on my family's dinner table and it was a custom that went back for many generations. I guess that Trione Winery, founded by my sons in 2008, can be regarded as the end-piece of all this vintage history.

It was a long time coming. We began with vineyards, bought another winery with Italian roots, sold part of it, bought it back, sold it again and finally, in 2008, put the family name on the labels of some very good Sonoma County varietals. I suppose, in some way, I was always open to the idea of a winery. I don't have to tell you that Italians, like all Southern Europeans, consider wine as simply a part of their diet. Years ago, a French restaurant in San Francisco had painted on its wall: "A dinner without wine is like a day without sun." I could not agree more.

After World War I, America engaged in what would come to be known as the Great Experiment, ratifying the 18th Amendment to the Constitution, which prohibited the manufacture and sale of alcoholic beverages. To the great surprise of many immigrants, this included wine.

There was, however, language in this new law which was known as Prohibition that allowed families to make a maximum of 200 gallons of wine per year for their own domestic use. Immigrant families, like mine, took full advantage of this "escape clause."

My father had a room in the basement of our house in Berkeley where he kept all the necessary equipment to make his quota. There were barrels, a fermentation vat, bottling equipment and an ample supply of bottles and corks. The crushing season was a social time for family and friends, when the immigrant families came together to help each other make their year's supply of wine. Of course, what was made had to be consumed. And it wasn't always

~ 90 ~

delectable. The immigrants, remember, had left their elders in Italy and many lacked experience in the fermentation process and sanitation against bacteria. Some of those Prohibition vintages were nearly intolerable.

Still, home winemaking was a healthy industry. And it can be credited with saving the grape growers of the North Bay and the Central Valley. In Emeryville, in San Francisco's East Bay, in the right season, there were dozens of freight cars full of grapes from Napa, Sonoma and the Fresno area. Buyers would walk the tracks and make their selections, averaging one or two tons. A ton of grapes would produce approximately 150 gallons of wine. Growers were also sending railcars full of grapes to eastern cities where they were in great demand from the large immigrant populations.

The transcontinental journey for the grapes each fall exposed them to extremes of heat and cold. In an attempt to help the grapes endure this period of delay, they were often picked and shipped prematurely when the brix (measurement of sugar) was below the acceptable amount. The condition of these grapes when sold was usually poor. In the hands of inexperienced vintners, they produced inferior quality wine, a harsh and sour product which came to be known, not flatteringly, as "Dago Red."

My early interest in wines was casual. In my college and Navy years, I always enjoyed wines, whatever the origin. And, with only a few boutique wineries in Napa and Sonoma counties, most of the table wines available came from the Central Valley of California. There were two basic types: red and white.

After World War II, when I sought to establish myself in some vocation, I took a position as trainee with E&J Gallo Winery of Modesto. Owned by brothers Ernest and Julio Gallo, who came from a family of winegrowers, it ranked as one of the largest wine companies in the world.

I didn't stay with Gallo. As I described in Chapter Five, I quit when they wanted me to relocate to Atlanta, Georgia, to become their southeast representative. But I did add a little to my basic awareness of wine.

Apart from the immigrant population, wine was not a popular

drink. Annual wine consumption per capita in the United States at the time I worked for Gallo was approximately 1.5 gallons, compared to Italy and France where each person's consumption was in excess of 18 to 20 gallons per year. There were many areas in this country – the southern states and parts of the mid-west – where wine simply didn't exist. Even in California, one didn't see the variety of wines on grocery store shelves we see today. Liquor stores or direct sales at wineries were generally the only retail outlets. At smaller wineries in Sonoma County – and I presume in Napa, as well – customers could bring a jug to the winery and the vintner would fill it for not much money.

By the 1960s, the interest in wines had begun to grow. While the generic reds and whites were still the most popular, budding connoisseurs began to take an interest in varietals. Eventually, consumers would differentiate and choose – often pairing with food – from cabernet sauvignon, zinfandel, pinot noir, merlot, chardonnay, sauvignon blanc and others.

Sonoma County, where grape growers had struggled in the years after Prohibition, enjoyed what might be called a Wine Renaissance. It began in the early 1970s with a few entrepreneurs who brought fortunes from other ventures to invest. The combination of premium wine, acres of vineyard and country living were hard to resist, giving rise to the adage that the way to make a small fortune in the wine business was to start with a big one. Wine became a familiar topic for the media. A new class of journalists called "wine writers" produced columns and published newsletters. There was a very popular film with Rock Hudson, called "This Earth is Mine," made in the Napa Valley – a love story in the vineyards, you might say.

Another important factor was a 1976 event that came to be known as "The Judgment of Paris." A British wine judge named Steven Spurrier, who had a shop in Paris where he sold only French wines, arranged a judging putting California chardonnays in competition with those from Burgundy and California cabernets with the best of France's Bourdeaux. Spurrier intended to put to rest any suggestion that California wines were even competitive, so he invited a reporter for Time magazine to witness the French triumph.

The chardonnays came first and even the judges were stunned when the blind tasting ended and a wine made by Chateau Montelena in the Napa Valley, from grapes grown in Sonoma County, beat all competitors.

Spurrier was reportedly so shocked and so concerned over these results that he "leaked" to the judges of the red wines that some were from California. With that information, some of the judges began to make snide remarks about the wines they tasted, criticizing what they were sure were the California entries – with the Time writer making notes.

When the blind tasting was over and the winner was revealed, they found that a cabernet made by Stags' Leap Winery in the Napa Valley had been judged the best, beating a wine that was among the most famous of French vintages, a Chateau Mouton Rothschild. It was, a writer for the Wall Street Journal termed it, "a vinous shot heard round the world." Nowadays, my grandchildren would say that the news "went viral." The Paris tasting turned out to be the landmark event that established the reputation of California wines – and, more specifically, the wines of Napa and Sonoma.

This prompted me, as further substantiation of my interest in wines, to take a correspondence course offered by the California Wine Institute, a trade cooperative financed by California wineries to educate interested people in the background of wines. I wasn't the only one who paid attention. National corporations, looking to diversify, began looking at what we now call "Wine Country" as an investment prospect. Much of this interest was short-lived. In many cases, after a time, the captains of industry became disillusioned with the rate of return and disposed of their investments – one way or another.

Schlitz Brewing Company of Milwaukee was one of these. In the 1960s and '70s, Schlitz was the most popular American beer. It was, you remember, "the beer that made Milwaukee famous," with the slogan "When you're out of Schlitz, you're out of beer." It was comparable to – larger, even – than Anheuser-Busch is today. The Uihlein family, owners of Schlitz, acquired the Geyser Peak Winery in 1972, even before the Paris tasting created a surge in the market. Located at Geyserville in northern Sonoma County, it had been founded in 1880 and through the years had been not only a winery but a brandy distillery. More recently, the Bagnani family had made not only wine there but wine vinegar – the popular Four Monks brand.

At the time the Uihlein family purchased the winery, production was at a minimum. They improved the facilities, which was a substantial investment, and acquired vineyard acreage, including 80 acres in Alexander Valley, two miles south of Geyser Peak. Those 80 acres were the site of the old, established Nervo Winery built in 1908. The acquisition of that old stone building and surrounding vineyards would prove very important to my family as 36 years later, after a series of transactions I will call "interesting" for lack of a better word, they would become my sons' Trione Winery.

I knew Robert Uihlein. I had played polo with him in Chicago. At the time, his two sons were playing polo, as were Victor and Mark, and I had even attempted, at one time, to arrange a family match, but for some reason or another it did not materialize. The Uihleins had ambitious plans for Geyser Peak. They were busily acquiring grape contracts with local growers. With the prospects of a grape buyer that could be counted on, my family and I began buying vineyards. In the course of a few years in the '70s, with the guidance of longtime Healdsburg grape grower Martin Frost, we acquired the River Road Ranch, a ranch in Hopland and the Cloverdale Ranch. We were in the grape business, big-time.

Unfortunately, Schlitz wasn't as good at wine as it had been at beer (their brewery was also in financial trouble at this point). The first vintage of the cabernet sauvignon was, to be kind, mediocre. Since the Uihlein purchase of Geyser Peak and Schlitz's plans for the winery had been widely publicized, the tarnished reputation spread quickly and didn't go away.

In an attempt to increase sales, the management initiated "wine in a box." This bore the Summit label and was the first attempt at this kind of merchandising. It was, and is, five liters of wine in a plastic bladder, inside a cardboard box, with a spigot. The collapsing bladder kept the wines from aerating as they were consumed. It provided a very practical way of storing wines, generally in a refrigerator, and provided wines to the consumer at a very nominal price.

Most of these wines were made from grapes from the Central Valley where prices were very low in comparison to Sonoma County. As a grower of premium grapes, I was friendly with the management of Geyser Peak. And, from time to time, the prospect of owning a winery would cross my mind. At one of our lunch meetings, I recall saying that if Schlitz ever wanted to sell the winery, its management should let me know. Meanwhile, Schlitz Brewery's reputation and popularity dropped substantially – the consequence, I believe, of an ill-advised marketing scheme.

Stroh Brewery of Detroit, headed by Peter Stroh, staged a successful, unfriendly acquisition of Schlitz, over strong objections from the Uihlein family. The takeover included not only the winery, but other assets such as a Coca-Cola franchise and real estate investments. Stroh was only interested in the marketing power Schlitz still had. They began liquidating non-brewery assets. One day, flying back from a Masonite board meeting in Chicago, I met Wayne Downey, then manager of Geyser Peak. He was returning from a meeting with the Stroh management. It turned out to be a significant encounter. "You might want to know," he said to me, "that Stroh has decided to sell the winery."

Stroh retained Bank of America in San Francisco because the bank had a department for sales and acquisitions. A very amiable man, John Fisher, supervised this department. The asking price for the winery, which included some 200 acres of vineyards plus an inventory of several thousand gallons of wine, was $14 million. My own assessment was that the assets had a value of approximately $16 million, at the very least. One misjudgment I made, I discovered later, was giving the wine inventory a "fresh wine" value. Much of the white wines were older and losing their full value. Before I agreed to the purchase, we were at a concert of the San Francisco Symphony. I noticed the concession stands were dispensing Summit wines in a box, from Geyser Peak. I checked and found that Geyser Peak was marketing over a million units of Summit wine in a box and less than 200 cases of conventional bottled varietals.

In the negotiation, we came to an acquisition price of $12 million. My credit line was inadequate to acquire this amount, so when Carl Reichardt, chairman of Wells Fargo, found that $12 million was the entire price of the winery, he insisted that I have some equity in the transaction. I had to provide $400,000 of my own funds. This was in 1983. By then I had already merged Sonoma Mortgage into Wells Fargo, Jim Laier and I had merged Molalla Forest Products into Masonite Corporation, and I had merged Summit Savings and Loan into Imperial Corporation of America.

At the age of 63, I acquired a new interest. It was at that time that Russell Green, a good friend who acquired and sold Simi Winery, said to a mutual friend, "Henry doesn't know it, but he's gone back to work." He was right. Within weeks of our acquisition of Geyser Peak, Wayne Downey resigned. He indicated ill health, but I suspected he merely wanted to retire. Wayne had been placed in control of the winery by Stroh to increase sales in every manner, as he had with the Coca-Cola franchise.

The controller, who had minimal marketing experience, took over as manager. There would be two more managers before we took a partner in the business – Penfolds Wines, the largest winery in Australia. Penfolds agreed to purchase 50 percent ownership of Geyser Peak for $10 million. Penfolds was part of a corporation called Tooth & Co., which, in turn, was owned by a five-corporation syndicate.

The president of Penfolds was Ian Mackly. We soon established a good rapport. We met quarterly, alternating between Geyser Peak winery and Australia. The trips to Australia became family events, which we enjoyed immensely. I remember Ian's comment during one of our early meetings. "Henry," he said, "the first thing we have to do is make good wines." We reorganized, with Daryl Groom,

Penfolds' bright, young winemaker in charge of red wine. We added 10 rotary processing tanks, thus reducing the fermentation period substantially. The rotary tanks also processed the skin and pulp in a way that reduced the tannin in the character of the wine. We also acquired 1,000 oak barrels. These were necessary for the important aging process.

The relationship with Penfolds was very harmonious. We were still in a money-losing mode, but there were encouraging signs of improvement – even the occasional month when the winery operated in the black. Then, about three years after Penfolds' acquisition, a financial analysis in Sydney, Australia, reported disturbing news. The five corporations owning Tooth & Co. were significantly overvalued. The Australian banks financing the overall structure were concerned. They ordered the consortium to reduce the amount of their indebtedness as rapidly as possible. One of Tooth & Co.'s more saleable assets was Penfolds.

A beer company, called South Australian Brewery, made an acceptable offer for Penfolds. In the final negotiation between the directors of Penfolds and the brewery, the buyers indicated they wanted to wait on California – which meant Geyser Peak. They wanted more time to review the investment. The director of Tooth & Co. agreed.

Later, the director of South Australian told me that, had Tooth insisted they agree to the entire acquisition, he would have. But a month later, after reviewing the Geyser Peak investment, he concluded they were not interested in any foreign investments. He declined to accept the acquisition of Geyser Peak. This left Tooth & Co. with just one California investment – 50 percent interest in Geyser Peak. Being advised of this, we had an acquisition meeting with the director. We reacquired Penfolds' interest in the winery for $400,000, payable in three annual installments.

Because Geyser Peak was still in a poor earning mode, I decided to manage the winery myself. I assumed direct control. To have the necessary liquidity, we sold one vineyard in Sonoma Valley to a neighbor. I was always concerned that our heavy volume of wine in the box sales was in jeopardy. We were the primary distributor,

~ 97 ~

but Gallo Winery, or even a smaller company, could easily have taken over our market share, since most of the wine we used was purchased from Central Valley sources.

When Art Ciocca, manager and principal owner of The Wine Group in Modesto, offered to purchase our Summit wine box operation for $4 million, I accepted.

Without Summit, Geyser Peak sales dropped from 1.16 million cases to just 160,000 cases, initiating another re-organization. I prepared myself to spend my work week at the winery – until I was approached by Dennis Pasquini. Dennis had been with Sebastiani Winery in Sonoma. I don't know why he left. He did give Sebastiani as a reference and was somehow related to the family. I contacted Dick Cuneo, president of Sebastiani, whom I already knew. He said, "Oh, he will sell cases of wine."

This was all I needed to know, so Dennis became president of Geyser Peak. He immediately hired Mike Pendergast as sales manager. Controller Harry Ellis agreed to continue and Daryl Groom, our gift from Australia, stayed on as manager of wine production. Geyser Peak's reputation for making good wines grew. Daryl was highly regarded in the wine community and Pasquini was as aggressive as promised. Nevertheless, in an effort to create incentives for the management team of Pasquini, Pendergast, Groom and Ellis, I verbally agreed to give them a 10 percent interest in the company. In order to keep the winery separate from our 800 acres of vineyards, my sons Victor and Mark established a sub chapter S corporation, jointly owned, called Vimark, which included all the vineyard acreage.

Our major distributor, through many of the states in the country, was Southern Wines & Spirits. They were also the exclusive distributors of Jim Beam bourbon whiskey. Jim Beam was owned by Fortune Brands, listed on the New York Stock Exchange. Fortune Brands was the former American Tobacco Company, makers of Lucky Strike cigarettes. The tobacco business had been sold to a British company and, with this substantial infusion of funds, the name had been changed to Fortune. Fortune Brands was vested in a variety of interests, including Titleist golf balls and Moen hardware as well as Jim Beam and others.

At a meeting with Southern Wine & Spirits, Rich Reese, president of Jim Beam, indicated his company was interested in buying a winery. I was told that the vice president of Southern responded, "The best winery you could buy is Geyser Peak." This set the stage for our negotiations with Fortune Brands. They retained an acquisition firm to negotiate for them. We retained the same people who had represented Stroh Brewery when we bought Geyser Peak.

The first issue was to establish an asking price. We decided to take the price-earnings ratios of publicly traded wineries, which, at the time, included the Napa giants Beringer and Mondavi, and apply those figures to Geyser Peak's earnings over the previous year. That way, we could establish a satisfactory asking price. In most instances, the price-earnings ratio was in excess of 10 times the annual earnings amount. Geyser Peak earnings were abnormally high because of the quality and volume of bulk wine Daryl Groom had sold to other wineries at a very good profit. The accepted formula produced an asking price of $105 million dollars. This method of pricing a privately held company was one a corporation executive could understand. In the final negotiations, we arrived at a price of $100 million for the winery and $5 million for the land around the winery.

We kept all the other acreage including the site of the Nervo Winery, which was then known as Canyon Road, the name of Geyser Peak's second label. We were prepared to accept an exchange of stock. Fortune Brands, however, would benefit financially from a cash sale. So, the transaction was made in cash. In the final negotiation, $10 million was allocated to the management team, $4 million to Pasquini and $2 million each to Ellis, Groom and Division Manager Gary Salankey. The cash disadvantage to them was the immediate tax liability, as distinguished from a transfer of stock.

After the sale, four regional managers contended Pasquini had promised them a share as well. This had been done without my knowledge or consent. The issue came to a jury trial. We prevailed, but at a cost of $700,000 in attorneys' fees. This concluded my financial interests in wines.

In 2007, Victor and Mark financed the construction of a new small winery on the Canyon Road site, adjoining picturesque 100-year-old Nervo Winery. Trione Winery was completed in 2008. Small amounts of select grapes of each varietal were allocated to Trione Winery from Vimark Vineyards. Victor and Mark hired Scot Covington, an excellent winemaker. They are producing a popular Bordeaux blend called, simply, Red Wine, as well as a cabernet sauvignon, syrah, sauvignon blanc, pinot noir, chardonnay and, the most recent addition, zinfandel. The wines are priced in the middle of the varietal wine categories, from $20 to $70 a bottle, and the future looks promising. Denise Trione Hicks, Mark's daughter, my granddaughter, is the marketing director.

Naturally, her grandfather was chomping at the bit, as an old polo player would say, to make suggestions. I must say that Denise has been very gentle in politely ignoring my advice. In an effort to control my enthusiasm, she and my sons gave me a fancy, engraved business card identifying me as a consultant.

When Denise made the presentation, I said, "Thank you for the honor. How many free cases of wine come with this?"

"None," she said, "You pay like the rest of us do."

So I pay. And I am one of their most aggressive customers.

CHAPTER XII ~ THE OAKLAND RAIDERS

Like so many adventures in my lifetime, owning a piece of the Oakland Raiders was an experience that started almost as a whim and blossomed into an interesting and profitable investment. In the 1950s, Sonoma Mortgage did business with Wayne Valley, a prominent homebuilder in the San Francisco Bay Area. Under the name of Braddock, Logan & Valley, he built several developments following World War II. Our company actively solicited mortgage contracts with builders and BLV was a good client. In addition to our business contacts, Wayne, his wife Gladys, and my wife, Madelyne, and I became good friends.

Wayne was a graduate of the University of Oregon, and was always interested in football. It was he who initiated the idea of developing a professional team in Oakland to compete in the newly formed American Football League. The San Francisco 49ers, then as now, played in the National Football League, and the Bay Area, he felt, could support a second pro team.

Wayne, as a matter of policy, generally looked for partners in his business ventures, though he was certainly capable of providing financing on his own merit. For the football franchise – the name Oakland Raiders had not yet been chosen – he invited several developers and contractors to join him. He asked me if I would be interested.

In 1959 and '60, Sonoma Mortgage was doing well but I had no excess funds for speculation on a football team. Besides, polo was my game. But I saw this as an opportunity to develop a closer relationship with other developers and homebuilders who were investors in the football franchise. I also believed that this venture would help cement a relationship with Valley's corporation. So I signed on.

My initial investment was to be a maximum of $50,000, for which I set up a line of credit. The agreement was that if the needs of the team operation were less, the money would not be used. In the first years, the amount needed was always at the maximum. Home

~ 101 ~

games with other AFL teams were played on the Frank Youell Field of Oakland High School. Seating was limited and ticket sales were never adequate to cover costs. Television rights were non-existent. Many of the initial investors withdrew their interests.

The prospects weren't great, but rather than collapse the project, Valley restructured the partnership so that he and another builder, Ed McGah, would be the general partners. Others would be limited partners, for which there were several who were eager to participate. I originally agreed to a 20 percent investment, but there were so many takers for his limited offer that I settled for 10 percent.

Coaches were always under Valley's supervision. In 1963, Al Davis was hired as head coach. A native New Yorker, he had played college football and, before becoming head coach in Oakland, had been an assistant coach with the San Diego Chargers. Under Davis, the team took on an encouraging and positive attitude, winning more games than before. After the team played for three years on the high school field, the Oakland City Council agreed to the construction of a real, professional-sized stadium. In 1966, the Oakland Raiders had their first game in their own home, to be known as the Oakland Coliseum.

I should add here that the name Oakland Raiders was adapted from one of the short stories written by that old oyster pirate Jack London. The team's logo was a pirate with an eye patch and typical pirate garb. Jack London's work seemed like the logical place to find a name. He had gone to school in Oakland and is honored there with several monuments including a waterfront tourist area near downtown known as Jack London Square.

We probably felt a greater affinity for London than the other investors since London's Beauty Ranch, where he built his ill-fated "Wolf House," in Glen Ellen, in the Valley of the Moon, is just 20 minutes from where we live and where I am writing this memoir. Beauty Ranch, where London died at age 40, is now a state park.

With the new Coliseum, attendance at games increased, as did the return on our investments. In 1966, Davis was offered the position of commissioner of the American Football League, just as Pete Rozelle headed the National League. Davis accepted, left his coaching job and took on the new adventure. However, within a year, the NFL and the AFL were consolidated. Perhaps because of seniority, Rozelle prevailed and Davis was terminated. It was then that Valley called all the partners together. He didn't ask us, he told us, that the general partners would be increased to three: himself, Ed McGah and Davis, who would become managing general partner. Along with the partnership came 10 percent of the franchise.

In the following years, the team, under Davis' supervision and John Madden's coaching, enjoyed great success, playing in no less than four Super Bowls. In 1968 the team's 13-1 record was the best in AFL history. In '68, in the nation's second Super Bowl, the Raiders lost to the Green Bay Packers but earned rings as AFL champions. Nine years later, they beat the Minnesota Vikings, in 1981 they won over the Philadelphia Eagles and in 1984 they beat the Washington Redskins. That's three super bowl rings in all.

In February of 1985, Wayne and his wife, Gladys, were flying down to Palm Springs with Madelyne and me. That very morning he had received a copy of a memorandum signed by McGah and Davis, literally giving Davis control of the club. Valley was livid. Why McGah signed was not known. He basically had no interest in football. We felt he had signed the memorandum without reading it.

Several times, Valley attempted to get Davis to revise the contract, without results. Lawyers became involved. The matter came before the Superior Court of Alameda County and the Honorable Judge Forrest Statz. Statz ruled for Davis. At this point, Valley gave up. He sold his interest to Davis. Since I had testified against Davis in my deposition for the court case, I decided to offer my shares to Davis, as well. Davis, however, made it clear he would not give me the same price he gave Valley. He had paid a premium price to have Valley out of the organization.

A few days later, Valley called to ask me not to accept the reduced price. His two partners in the BLV homebuilding company, Braddock and Logan, also wanted to sell their shares and didn't want their selling position threatened with a lower sale price. So I did nothing. I remained a limited partner as the team continued under the total control of Al Davis.

There were plenty of perks for the partners. We could fly with the team to games at other cities, wives included. There was a pretty fancy clubroom set up in the Coliseum for the owners and guests and visiting celebrities to enjoy before and during games. All this "insider" luxury, plus the positive financial position of the franchise, kept all of the partners quite satisfied, myself included.

I remember, however, one less-than-happy moment that occurred on the Oakmont golf course. It was pure coincidence that Judge Forrest "Bud" Statz, who had ruled in favor of Al Davis many years before, had been hired as the first dean of our Empire Law School when he retired from the Alameda County bench. On this day, he happened to be playing just ahead of my foursome, which included Wayne Valley. I didn't think about it, but Wayne did. "See that fellow ahead?" he said to us. "He cost me the Oakland Raiders."

When Davis first became coach, I was able to encourage him to have the team hold their summer practice in Santa Rosa. El Rancho Tropicana was a well-established motel and conference complex at the south edge of town – with a large acreage suitable for practice fields behind it. There were meeting rooms and dining facilities to accommodate the players and staff during those weeks of pre-season workouts. To me, it was a satisfaction. The city was pleased with the arrangement and it continued for nearly 20 years. But this Santa Rosa sojourn couldn't last forever. In 1982 the Raiders moved to Los Angeles for 12 years, and our town's close relationship with its "boys of summer" came to an end.

When the Raiders had agreed to use the Oakland Coliseum in 1965, the city's leaders demanded much from the Raider management in return for the use of the new facility. Revenue from parking and rental of space for concessions were retained by the city. When the time came to renegotiate the contract, the city council held fast and alienated the staff of the Raiders.

As it happened, the Los Angeles Rams had gone to St. Louis, and L.A., at the time, had no professional football team in the area. There was one attempt by the City of Industry to offer the Raiders a stadium, but it was unsuccessful. Then the commission that oversaw the venerable old Los Angeles Memorial Coliseum made an offer that included, among other things, income from booth profits. Davis agreed. The Raiders were going to Los Angeles.

I always felt the team was, in reality, the Northern California Raiders. Supporters came by busloads from every county north of the bay. By the early 1980s, when talk began of a move to L.A., I had participated in the Raiders' organization for 25 years. In addition to disappointment at the decision, I also was preoccupied by our acquisition of Geyser Peak Winery. I suppose you could say that I decided to "punt." I offered my shares to Davis at $1.86 million. It was a good profit on my investment – although it was peanuts compared to what pro football franchises are worth now.

Apparently, the marriage to the Los Angeles Coliseum didn't work as expected. By 1995, with new and favorable endorsements, the Raiders moved back to Oakland, where they are today. In the meantime, El Rancho had been closed and torn down to make way for a shopping mall. And I was no longer in the partnership to lobby for Santa Rosa as a training site. The training camp is now in Napa.

When the Raiders won three Super Bowls – XI, XV and XVIII – each owner and player received a handsome ring with his name engraved on the side. As the story goes, someone asked Al Davis why he designed such a flashy piece of jewelry, and he responded: "Well, if the ring bearer is visiting the Court of St. James, it's hoped that the Queen, in seeing it, would say, 'Wow, what a ring!'"

And she undoubtedly would. ❖❖❖

CHAPTER XIII ~ HOW I GOT MY RANGER HAT

I suppose, in a very roundabout way, you can credit Wayne Valley and the Oakland Raiders for my involvement in the creation of Annadel State Park and the State Park Foundation. In 1969, the Oakland developer, who had become a close friend and brought me to a partnership in the Raiders, had plans to create a second-home community on a large ranch property in the hills east of Santa Rosa. The 8,000 acres had been assembled in various parcels by an industrialist named Joe Coney, who called it Annadel Farms. Included was all the land that is now Oakmont and Wild Oak as well as Annadel State Park.

In the late 1960s, Coney sought to sell the very beautiful mountainous area south of Oakmont, some 5,100 acres including woodlands, pastures, a lake and trails. Valley formed a corporation he named Lakeworld and visualized a subdivision there with some 5,000 homes for 15,000 to 20,000 residents. He would offer 1,500 acres of open space, he said, three lakes, equestrian trails – all the amenities of Lake of the Pines, a similar community he had built in the Sierra foothills.

I was very familiar with Annadel. Coney had been generous about letting riding groups, like the Sonoma County Trail Blazers, stage their rides and annual encampments there. I knew how beautiful it was. And, as much as I liked Wayne, I felt the scale of his proposal was overwhelming. The land, bordering Santa Rosa on the east, seemed to me to be a perfect site for a park. Nor was I alone in this belief. The embryo conservationist movement in the community rallied to stop the development before it started, and the young city manager of Santa Rosa, Ken Blackman, could point out a thousand reasons why it was not a good idea, ending, as I recall, with, "Over my dead body!" The battle was joined. But before I describe what happened next, it seems important to provide some historical background.

According to local lore, the area in question had been named Annie's Dell by Irish immigrant Sam Hutchinson in honor of his eldest daughter. Hutchinson bought the land, the southwest

~ 106 ~

portion of Rancho Los Guilucos land grant, in 1871. The name would be shortened by time to Annadel. The Hutchinsons – Sam and his son Tom – ran cattle, raised hops and had a profitable quarrying industry on the property, which contained deposits of a basalt-type stone that was cut into blocks to pave the streets of San Francisco and Oakland. The spolls, or chips of the stonecutters' work, can still be seen at the several quarry sites along the ridge.

When Joe Coney purchased the land in the 1930s, he was secure in the ranks of rich industrialists. A naval architect by profession, he had designed destroyers in World War I and parlayed his skills into a fleet of oil tankers in partnership with Stanley Hiller Sr., known as Hillcone Steamship Co. Coney's investments included some 3.5 million acres in South America, with gold, silver and tungsten mines. Always seeking new ventures, he experimented with a new form of cement and lost a million dollars on a fleet of fishing boats and a processing plant in Newfoundland.

He was nothing if not colorful. Annadel Farms became a diversion from his business interests. It was, more or less, his summer retreat. It was well stocked with horses and cattle. He planted more hop vines and built a dryer. And, with his Midas touch, Coney discovered deposits of perlite, a volcanic mineral used in both horticulture and industry.

Joe, who lived to be over 103 years old, was a hospitable host, allowing horsemen and friends to enjoy the vast area with its many trails and its lake. From the ranch's high elevations, everyone enjoyed the views of the surrounding area. Besides the Trail Blazers and other riding groups, Boy Scouts and Girl Scouts took advantage of Coney's welcome. He also allowed military units – the Marines, the National Guard – to hold maneuvers in the remote areas. The large 100-acre lake on the very top of the ranch he christened Lake Ilsanjo, a hybrid of his and his wife Ilse's names. What happened to Coney's idyllic estate is chronicled in historian Simone Wilson's book entitled "Wild Oak, Past and Present."

Coney enjoyed his land for more than 30 years. But fortunes change and assessments and taxes rise. Coney had invested in a huge ranch in Argentina, a ranch that an Argentine polo acquaintance of mine told me was "bigger than the state of Rhode Island." He had some issues with the Argentine government over property matters and, when he was told that he could solve them by buying the government official a new American car, he rebelled, saying that he wouldn't participate in such dealings. As a result, he lost the Argentine investment.

And, here at home, Coney's property taxes, according to Wilson, rose 700 percent in the early '60s, prompting him to sell, in '63, the former hop yard along Highway 12. The buyer was H.N. "Nor" Berger of Fairfield Homes in the Sacramento Valley, who created a state-of-the-art retirement community, built around a golf course. Known as Oakmont, it has since been sold and increased in size and amenities. It is included in the Santa Rosa city limits and has a population of more than 5,000.

Coney, still strapped for cash, mortgaged the remainder of the land and, in the mid-'60s, began planning a development in the hills, an ambitious project with several thousand homes and a golf course. He sought a developer to partner with and found Valley who took a half-million dollar option on the land, allowing him to buy the entire 5,100 acres if Coney couldn't pay the mortgage. In 1969 he defaulted and Valley became the sole owner of Annadel, with his own big plans for the development he called Santa Rosa Lakes. As I have suggested, I had other ideas, which were supported by the City of Santa Rosa and Manager Blackman. With the imposition of requirements for underground utilities, lighting and sewer, Valley forfeited his option money on the ranch and abandoned the project.

Several years earlier, when I was a vice president of the Bay Area Council, I had met William Penn Mott. He was director of the East Bay Regional Park District and was later appointed director of California's Division of Beaches and Parks by Governor Ronald Reagan. His administration was most commendable. In those days, the state had abundant funds for additions to the park system, which was recognized as one of the finest in the country. When Reagan's term expired, Jerry Brown became governor. He made a political appointment and Mott resigned.

In order to assure the continued health of the park system, a group of interested citizens including Joe Long, founder of Long's Drug Stores, and East Bay builder Robert Nahas, another early investor in the Raiders, were exploring ways to aid the parks. As it happened, I ran into Long from time to time because his duck club was next to mine in the Butte Sink. In a casual conversation with Joe, I mentioned the Annadel property and its desirability as a park. I recall the price placed on Joe Coney's land was $5 million.

Long told me that there was a source of federal money that would pay for half of the acquisition price of proposed parklands. When former state director Mott organized the California State Parks Foundation in 1969, Annadel was the foundation's first project. With Long and Nahas and several others, I became a board member of the foundation and the first chairman, a position I held for 14 years.

The state park system then had 86 parks extending from the Oregon border, along the coast, through Southern California to the Mexican border. It needed an auxiliary type of non-profit foundation that could further supplement the needs of the park system with funds and non-government assistance. This is exactly what happened with the Coney property. With my sons, I optioned the property from Valley. Through the embryo foundation, we got a promise of $2 million from the U.S. Department of Interior in the form of a grant that needed to be matched.

We then began the long haul to find the necessary matching funds to buy California a new park named Annadel.

The complex financial details of the Annadel purchase are in a history of the park written by Verna Mays and published in the September 1979 issue of *Sonoma Business* magazine. I will attempt a summary, which I'm sure is over-simplified. The funding process took several years. My family and the Trione Foundation made an initial contribution of about $300,000. Four pieces on the fringe of the proposed park were split off and sold. This was unusual, but the contour of the land, according to Foundation Director Mott, made it possible without disturbing the integrity of the park. Bill

~ 109 ~

Mott was later selected to become Director of the National Park Service, supervising all federal parks in the nation. But he got our California foundation off to a successful start.

In "rounding the corners of the ranch," about 10 acres at the northwest corner, off Summerfield Road, were sold to J. Ralph Stone, whose Santa Rosa S&L had been acquired by Great Western Savings. My sons, Victor and Mark, purchased 400 acres that is now the Wild Oak residential area, the polo field and the parcel that contained Joe Coney's house. In addition, the City of Santa Rosa owned two excess lots, which it sold and applied that money to the matching fund.

Meanwhile, a community group was organized by the City Council to raise money from the general public. The Friends of Annadel, headed by physician Brad Lundborg and advertising and public relations executive Alan Milner, raised some $16,000. Other donations came from Hewlett-Packard and the National Audubon Society. To make up a shortage, I donated another $250,000, bringing my total "investment" in this park, including the option, to more than $1 million. Since title to the parkland passed to the State of California, I have never regretted a penny of it.

The Annadel State Park now has 40 miles of trails on Santa Rosa's eastern flank. It is enjoyed by horseback riders, bicyclists and hikers who can enter at the city's Howarth Park on Summerfield Road, pass through Sonoma County's Spring Lake Park and into Annadel, travelling more than 15 miles in a relatively straight path, before leaving parkland at Kenwood. It is recognized as one of the most heavily used parks in the state.

When California's state parks experienced serious deficit problems in 2012, the state planned to close 70 parks, including Annadel. The very idea of "closing" Annadel was something of a bad joke since it was far from a single-entrance park facility. With so much land and so many trails, users can enter Annadel from all sides. The danger, course, was that there would be no management of the many thousands of hikers, horseback riders and bicyclists who considered the park part of Santa Rosa's backyard.

Sonoma County Regional Parks' director Caryl Hart, who also serves on the State Park and Recreation Commission, felt the county could do a good job of managing the park, if the funds could be raised. When Caryl called me, I agreed and put up $100,000 that was matched and more by private donations. In all, the county raised about $400,000 and took over the management, with the state contributing $50,000 and a ranger.

Meanwhile the state parks had a "found money" episode and have been able to provide more rangers and more funding. The state was able to take back management of the park in July of 2013.

Back at the ranch, we organized the Wild Oak Saddle Club, in 1975, using the Coney home as a clubhouse. The original saddle club was a group of riders, mostly Trail Blazers, but it has expanded to include a large social component. Joe Coney's old house still has some good parties.

Three years ago, I was designated chairman emeritus of the California State Parks Foundation. There are now 47 active board members and 23 full-time employees. This is a far cry from the 100-square-foot office in Oakland's Tribune Tower, where Bill Mott began the organization.

In June of 2008, at the California State Parks Foundation's annual meeting at South Lake Tahoe, the California State Park Rangers Association awarded me the title of Honorary California State Park Ranger. With this recognition came a State Park Ranger's felt hat.

My friends know how much I like hats. And this one is special. It is a very distinctive broad-brimmed hat, often identified as a "Teddy Roosevelt" or "Rough Rider" hat. It is worn by all rangers on duty. I enjoy wearing it on appropriate occasions. ❖❖❖

PHOTOGRAPHS
Circa 1957 ~ 2013

Sonoma Mortgage's new home on Fourth Street, Santa Rosa, in 1957.
The IRS was our tenant.

Redwood like this made
Mollala Forest Products
a successful venture.

Australian Colin Hensen
and I talk wine and
business in 1989.
~ *Jeff Kan Lee*
for *The Press Democrat*

Where Empire College began. Madelyne chose the name for this historic building on Courthouse Square when we gilded the tower and fixed the clock in the 1960s.
~ *John LeBaron for The Press Democrat*

Much credit for the success of Empire College is due to my colleague Dorothe Hutchinson, who was president and chairman of the board in the school's growing years. She was succeeded as president by Roy Hurd.

Empire College's current home on Cleveland Avenue where more than 1,000 students study business and law.

A trio of Trail Blazers. Victor
to my left, Mark on the right.

Setting a fast pace
for my sons.

Vic and Mark lead off a trail ride. 1978

Polo was very important in my life. This white mare, called Sweetheart, was a favorite.

There have been many chances for "action" photos on the Wild Oak polo field.

Curly Ramos and me with the ponies.

My greatest fan, Madelyne, introduces her Corgi, Willie, to my mare, Sweetheart.

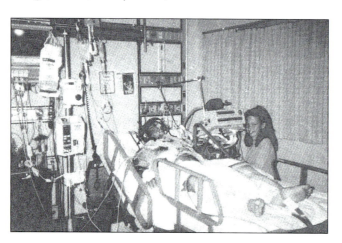

My polo career came to an abrupt halt in 1990 when I was gravely injured in a trail ride accident. I spent many weeks in Memorial Hospital. My granddaughter, Sally, who grew up to be a nurse, is at my side in this photo.

Three Super Bowl rings and an AFC Championship ring are impressive souvenirs of my early investment in the Oakland Raiders.

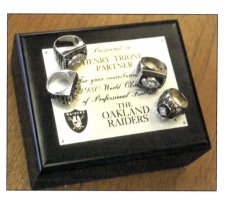

My friend Ralph Stone and I prepare for the first Truffle Congress in Santa Rosa in 1975.
~ *Joe Price Jr. for The Press Democrat*

In 1984 I was honored to accept a Gravenstein apple seedling from the original Russian orchard at Fort Ross from William Penn Mott of the California State Parks Foundation.
~ *Jeff Kan Lee for The Press Democrat*

Joe Coney's weekend house at Annadel was the scene of many good times.

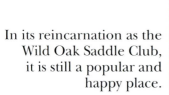

In its reincarnation as the Wild Oak Saddle Club, it is still a popular and happy place.

The "jolly boys:" With Mark, grandson Hank and Victor.

Staying in tune: Proving that a former "Northwest Night Rider" can still make music.

The Tule Goose Duck Club, scene of many a good hunt and convivial gathering.

I am very proud of my part in creating the "Lone Sailor" memorial honoring the men and women of the U. S. Sea Services.

In 1983, the new chapel at Memorial Hospital was named St. Catherine's for my mother. The family gathered for the dedication. To my right: Madelyne, Victor, Kathy and Mark with grandson Hank and granddaughter Denise in front.
~ *SR Memorial Hospital*

I take my turn with the shovel at the ground-breaking for Star of the Valley Church in July of 1983. With me are, left to right, John Doolittle, Roz (Rosalind) Murphy, and Msgr. Gerard Fahey. Behind me is Charlie O'Callaghan.

In South Africa on a visit to Masonite plants, Madelyne and I lunched in the restaurant at the famous Cecil Rhodes Memorial in Cape Town. Circa 1977.

Eileen and me on our wedding day in 2006 with her sons, Kevin, Jim and John Ryan.

The Trione family. Christmas, 2013.

CHAPTER XIV ~ MY LIFE WITH HORSES

One glorious weekend day in the 1960s, several of us would-be cowboys were riding at the Sonoma County Fairgrounds when a life-changing event occurred. Bob Walter put me up on one of his polo ponies and put a mallet in my hand. It is no exaggeration to say that I was hooked from my first swing.

It may have been the annual Fortuna Rodeo that was the start of my fascination with horses. This event was way more important than the town itself in the ranks of western riders. In the 1930s, my friends and I would be the first on hand, to sit on the corral fences and admire the horses – bucking broncos included – as they arrived from all over the western states for this summer event.

Occasionally, some friend of my family would allow me to ride one of his ranch horses in the hills of Humboldt County. It was pure pleasure. Later, when the Navy stationed me at the Alameda Air Station, I liked to spend a Sunday on occasion at Golden Gate Park, watching the polo matches. Little did I think then that in a few years I would have the opportunity to play there – even play with some of the men I watched during the war, like L.C. Smith, Bill Gilmore and Bob Skene.

When we moved to Santa Rosa, I acquired my first horse, an average-sized sorrel named Pinky. He had an easy single-foot gait that made it an extra pleasure to ride on the trails. Years before World War II, even as far back as 1935, a group of Sonoma County men had formed a drill team they called the Sonoma County Cavaliers. Their standard uniform was a white western hat, red corduroy shirt and blue jeans. They achieved a certain degree of regional fame, riding regularly at the Sonoma County Fair and the California State Fair in Sacramento and performing at the World's Fair on Treasure Island in 1939. Pinky and I were fortunate to join them, and for years we enjoyed being part of the performances and parades.

Sometime in the 1950s, I was invited to become a Trail Blazer. This riding club's "trek" was – and is – a rite of late spring for the

~ 113 ~

North Coast horsemen. The five-day trip in early June involved several hundred local riders. Each year they selected a route that led them from 20 to 25 miles each day for five days through the hills of Northern California. A "chuck wagon" and a culinary crew followed, as did a truck that carried the bedrolls. The bar, of course, was well supplied and all the entertainment and music came from within the group. In 1957, I was the secretary who carried the burden of all correspondence. In 1975, I was elected president.

As the years went by and the membership increased, both in number and in age, it was more convenient to have one central camp and ride out on day rides. This afforded the opportunity of a more sophisticated kitchen and more comfortable sleeping accommodations. The rides are still held. Today the Trail Blazers' membership is a maximum of 300, and there is always a waiting list of horsemen eager to come along.

I also became a member of the much-larger Rancheros Vistadores, a group of 1,000 or more riders, centered in Santa Barbara. They meet in May for a five-day ride from their permanent camp in the Santa Ynez Mountains, with a dining room and a hall for performances that were somewhat more polished than the Trail Blazers, since there were musicians and actors in the club, including Ronald Reagan. Because of the size of this group, it is broken up into several camps. I was a member of the 4QU2 camp. These camps are a little like college fraternities in that lifelong friendships are developed there. Another group of riders I joined was the Frontier Boys, a smaller contingent, perhaps 75 to 100 riders, that met to ride in northeastern California for four days each September.

And then polo came into my life. Bob Walter, the guy who put the mallet in my hand, was a highly rated polo player who had come to town not long before, when he and his wife, Mary Ellen, known as Mickey, bought the beautiful Fountaingrove Ranch at the north end of Santa Rosa.

The Walters, who came from Milwaukee, were part of a growing number of interesting people who were "discovering"

Sonoma County in those years. Mickey was the daughter of the chairman of the board of Briggs & Stratton engines. Bob was a cattleman as well as an established polo player, having played for years in Milwaukee summers and Florida winters. He had a five-goal rating, putting him at the top of his career and in the upper echelons of accomplished polo players. The Walters' Fountaingrove is now the site of an Agilent Technologies plant and several other major companies, as well as a Hilton hotel and a residential development.

The ranch had a unique history. In the 19th century it was the site of a Utopian community called Fountaingrove, led by a charismatic minister, writer and poet named Thomas Lake Harris, who established a winery there. Harris was succeeded by another interesting owner, a Japanese Samurai named Kanaye Nagasawa who was one of the first Japanese in the United States. Nagasawa continued wine production until his death in 1934 when the winery was purchased by Errol McBoyle, owner of the famous Empire Mine in Grass Valley in the Sierra foothills. By the time the Walters purchased the land from the estate of McBoyle's widow, the grapevines had been removed to make way for pastureland. It was ideal for Bob's polo ponies, which he brought with him from the east.

As the days and months and years went by, my interest in polo increased. Bob sold me two of his older ponies, ideal for a beginner. I constructed a "cage" at our home on Montecito Avenue and spent happy hours on a wooden mount that gave me space to swing and improve my skills with the mallet.

In the book entitled "As to Polo," the author's preface to his instructions for the sport stated it clearly: "One must never allow business or pleasure to interfere with one's polo." I took this to heart. Polo occupied almost all my spare moments from then on. My patient wife, Madelyne, sat on the sidelines for hours, praying I wouldn't fall off. She was most certainly bored to death watching a group of overgrown boys spending hours hitting a tennis-like ball up and down an area equal to the size of nine football fields.

On weekends in the winter months, we would fly down to Palm

Springs and play at Eldorado Polo Club. It was located where the Vintage Country Club of Palm Desert is now. By that time I had acquired five horses. With my demanding business schedule, I needed someone to care for the horses and keep them in good shape, which meant exercising them regularly and keeping the tack in good condition. There weren't a lot of people with polo pony experience available locally. But, through Bob Walter's connections, I was fortunate to find Jesse Ramos. Jesse, who was of Mexican descent, had grown up in Texas. He and his brothers were raised and trained to become managers of strings of polo ponies.

I purchased an 80-acre parcel of land on Fulton Road in West Santa Rosa for my horses. Jesse lived there. We developed a dirt polo field that was quite adequate for training and for "stick and ball," which is the phrase used for practicing. Jesse had a wife and family in Texas, whom he would visit on occasion. After two years, he decided he wanted to return to Texas. Fortunately for me, his son Sabas "Curly" Ramos was an equally experienced horseman.

Curly had married an Italian girl named Sophie he met in New York during his Korean War Army service. When he came to work for us, he and Sophie already had four children, two girls and two boys. Throughout all his remaining years, Curly managed our horse operation. He was a great friend and taught Victor and Mark how to play the game. Sophie died in the 1970s. After a year or so, Curly married Lynn. They were a very happy couple. Curly died of cancer in 2004. At his family's request, five of us took a small container of Curly's ashes and spread them on the polo field.

In the 1970s, I acquired an interest in the Eldorado Polo Club of Palm Springs. The Eldorado was a very informal group of congenial low-goal players run by Tony Veen, who had managed polo operations for the veteran L.C. Smith in the Bay Area before coming to the desert. Before I joined the group, the club's polo fields, near the Eldorado Golf & Country Club, were owned by developer David Bohannon and others. The club bought the land from the Bohannon group for $1,200 an acre. There were only

10 acres involved but it was contiguous to open space that was government land. We were able to use it without any objections.

The adjoining parcels were actually Homestead Act land, property where a citizen could stake a claim, live there for three years, improve it and take possession in fee. The size of a claim was 160 acres. Until World War I, veterans were given scrip for purchasing homestead land. Much of it, including most of the land contiguous to the polo club parcel, was still available for claim. Since scrip was the only way to acquire it, brokers made a market in this old scrip and exchanged it for land.

Two club members had contacted the government office in Riverside, hoping to purchase the land next door, but the Bohannon group got there first. An investor was already developing what became the Vintage Club and our 10-acre parcel was part of his plans. We were forced to sell. As I recall, the price was about $2,000 an acre.

We didn't give up on the polo club idea. We found available land in the La Quinta area, south of Indio, on 51st between Madison and Monroe. It was 120 acres of former orange grove that included a pretty little three-acre lake. It was ideal for our facilities, had adequate water and good soil for a polo field. The price was $1,700 an acre. Twenty of us purchased the land and, when an adjoining 60-acre parcel became available, we bought it as well – for $2,000 an acre. The Eldorado Club now had 180 acres suitable for six regulation-sized fields, plus stable area for at least 200 horses and a site for a clubhouse that overlooked the entire facility.

The original members who played a prominent part in the early development of the facility included Carlton Beal, Willis Allen, Charles Hetherington, Frank Yturria, Glen Holden, Paul Von Gontard, Mack Jason, and myself. Tony Veen was the first manager. When he retired, Alex Jacoy managed the club throughout the years. The enterprise was run by two boards of directors – one for the polo club and another for the land we called Lake Farms. The arrangement between the two entities was that the club paid an annual rental fee that approximated the taxes and insurance.

The polo club was responsible for maintenance. The season usually started in November, but the heaviest activity was, and is, from January to April. Members play regularly through the week, higher goal teams generally play on Sunday afternoons.

In addition to promoting the game of polo in Palm Springs, I supported participation in the game back home in Sonoma County as well.

About 1983, when I acquired Geyser Peak Winery near Geyserville, I started a Geyser Peak Seniors Tournament with a minimum player-age of 50 years. Teams were arranged by Alex Jacoy and Susan Stovall. With their knowledge of each player's experience, they matched the teams evenly. Through the years, the tournament grew to a dozen teams that played over a weekend each March.

We hosted a Saturday night dinner before the final match on Sunday. Each participant got a bottle of wine and a memento cap inscribed "Geyser Peak Winery Seniors," a different color each year. For many of the players, the cap became a collector's item. When we sold Geyser Peak Winery to Fortune Brands, we changed the formal name of the tournament to Trione Vineyards. With the formation of Trione Winery, "Trione Vineyards & Winery" became the logo on the cap.

Polo was new to Sonoma County but had a long history around the world. Argentina is generally known as the homeland of polo, although the sport actually originated in Asia centuries ago. The British acquired an interest in polo in their early occupation of India, but it is Argentina that is considered central to the sport. Today in California, we have five or six polo facilities. The environs around Buenos Aires have 30 or more polo fields. The Argentina Open draws the finest of players and an audience like the ones we have at our major football games.

Once, when in Argentina, I met Camillo Aldo, an active polo player and owner of a winery. We put together an annual match with the modest title "International Polo Tournament of The Great Wineries of the World." For several years in the 1980s and 1990s, we played in Argentina, Chile, Brazil, Italy, Mexico and once on our own fields in Santa Rosa. These were usually four-chukker events, very social – more in the nature of a golf match with friends. The rating of the teams was generally in the 3 to 4 goal range. After the matches there was a social hour that included tastings of the wines of all participants.

Putting a weekend together was not easy. Participants did not ship their own horses to the tournaments, so at least 40 extra horses were required. In Argentina and Chile, it was easy to find extra horses for the event. But in our case, we had to make our own participants provide horses for the visitors if they wanted to play.

The 10 acres that we had set aside from the Wild Oak subdivision has given us adequate acreage for a polo field. We also created an auxiliary field for "stick and ball" practice. With equipment and personnel available at Molalla Forest Products, we developed the fields. A modest home, contiguous to the existing barn, was adequate for Curly Ramos and his family. Curly developed and managed the fields until his death. Needless to say, the Wild Oak fields made it very convenient, indeed, for me to enjoy my favorite sport.

Fortunately, there were several good players in Santa Rosa, including Bud Dardi who owned the local McDonald's franchise and Pete Gilham Sr. and Pete Gilham Jr., owners of Cattlemens restaurants, and, of course, my two sons, Vic and Mark.

We have had lots of fun with our Santa Rosa polo. At one of our Sunday tournaments, the Cattlemens' Cowboys team, composed of Pete Gilham, Pete Gilham Jr. and two others, were competing against the Italian Stallions, consisting of Victor, Mark, Bud Dardi and myself. To add color, I had my helmet striped with red, white and green – the colors of the Italian flag – from one end to the other. Bud's helmet was three-quarters covered because he was one quarter Irish. Vic's and Mark's stripes went just halfway. I'm afraid I must admit that the Gilham team beat our red and green team 5-2. We submitted an account to the local newspaper (which was, of course, never printed). Our headline said "Italian Stallions Gelded by Cowboys."

Presently, the club is known as the Wine Country Polo Club. Polo is still played regularly from May to October with games scheduled on Thursdays, Saturdays and Sundays. There are about 25 members, mostly low-goal players. Women and men participate equally, which is a change that has occurred in the last half-century. The field maintenance is not inexpensive. We assumed it personally at first but as the polo club grew in size, it was able to support most of the costs.

Around the same time, we started the Wild Oak Saddle Club in Joe Coney's former residence in Santa Rosa. The Saddle Club, limited to a membership of 200, was originally a horsemen's club but has grown into a social club with many amenities including well-used card rooms, buffet lunches and dinners in the dining room or on the terrace with its sweeping view of Hood Mountain. Riders still meet each Wednesday and ride the adjoining Annadel Park.

I no longer play polo due to a riding accident in 1990. It was a Saturday in May. Dan Stamps and I went up to the Folded Hills Ranch near Yorkville with a two-horse trailer. Danny is my nephew-in-law, married to my sister's daughter, Valerie. The horses were stable mates. Mine was a polo pony, a mare named Ginger, I think, and Danny's was a trail horse, a gelding.

There were about 70 people on the ride, which was kind of a warm-up for the upcoming Trail Blazers' trek. Danny and I rode off together. Just up from the ranch, as we started up a steep trail, Dan's saddle slipped back and his horse bucked him off. He turned back to the ranch and when my mare saw her boyfriend going home, she wanted to go, too. She backed up and lost her footing and we went over an embankment, maybe 30 feet down into a rocky creek.

Bunny Comstock, who was riding behind us, said the last he saw of me I was in the stirrups but the horse and I were both upside down. I learned later that Bunny and Bill Nielsen and Ed Peterson jumped off their horses and down into the creek where I had landed – with the horse on top of me. I think the mare was unconscious for a short time and I guess I was as well.

The reins were around my neck and Bunny pulled them off, although I don't remember that. The mare was beginning to thrash around to get up as the boys pulled me out from under her.

Bob Bailey and Ed Healey, I'm told, had gone back to the ranch to call for help and Hunter Quistgard went to bring up his big SUV which they intended to use to haul me out of there. Fortunately, before they moved me, the crew from the Boonville Forestry Station arrived with the proper equipment.

They secured me, still lying flat, to a board. I must have been conscious because those who were there remember that the crew asked my age and I said 69, which was correct. In fact, I was about to turn 70 – my friend Ralph Stone whose birthday is the same as mine was turning 80, and I had planned a big, fancy "150th Birthday" party at the Pacific-Union Club in San Francisco. Needless to say, that event was cancelled.

I remember I had a nice new Levi jacket and when I was on that board they began to cut it off me and I protested that I could take it off, but they insisted that I was not to move my arms.

As it turned out, I had a broken neck, among other injuries, and their good care may well have saved my life. A helicopter came for me and took me to Santa Rosa Memorial Hospital and Madelyne was there, waiting.

I was more than a month at Memorial. I had broken my neck and virtually all of my ribs and I had a gash on my head that took many stitches to close. I still carry a scar on my forehead.

There were a few times when I didn't think I was going to make it. Most of what I remember about the first days was the dreams, the nightmares. I don't remember what they were about. It's probably just as well, but I can remember having them.

My hospital discharge summary listed not only my broken neck, which was very close to being paralyzing, but 18 rib fractures causing respiratory failure and the head wound.

My doctors later admitted that they really didn't give me much of a chance to make it. But I fooled them. I was on a respirator for two weeks and I had a brace for my neck, a contraption that was actually screwed into my skull. I wore that "halo" home when I finally left the hospital in late June and, in fact, I wore it on my first trips back to the office in mid-July and to social events, including our International Polo Championship matches at the Wild Oak polo field.

I did ride several times, many months after the accident. In May of '91, the first year anniversary of my "tumble," I went on the Trail Blazers' trek, at the same Folded Hills Ranch, for at least two days of the week-long encampment. But, in a follow-up visit to my doctor, he concluded his examination by saying, "I wouldn't fall off a horse again if I were you, Henry." Madelyne was with me. That ended my riding career.

My polo activity now is the management and maintenance of the polo fields and the club in Santa Rosa and being a dedicated spectator in both Santa Rosa and Palm Springs. My interest in the sport through the years motivated some good friends, namely Glen Holden, Geri and Bud Dardi and Madeline and Mack Jason, to nominate me for an award from the U.S. polo hall of fame in 2008. The induction ceremony was held in West Palm Beach, Florida, in March of that year. I was deeply honored by the designation.

Let me clarify: The Museum of Polo and Hall of Fame gives several awards each year – to horses, to outstanding polo players and to people who have contributed to polo in some way. The last category was mine.

So goes one of the more colorful parts of my life. Many fond memories and friendships from all over the world were a result of those years in the saddle. Playing with my sons on the same team is a very special memory. ❖❖❖

CHAPTER XV ~ TRIFLING WITH TRUFFLES

In April of 1974, Madelyne and I and our good friends Ralph and Lois Stone, with eight other couples we knew through the savings and loan business, sailed on the S.S. France for the first leg of its farewell world tour. We had all hoped to make it a true circumnavigation, but this was the only leg that had space for us. It was a memorable voyage from New York to Cannes. Through the influence of a member of our party, we enjoyed our own private dining room. During our final night together, each couple discussed their plans upon arrival.

One couple was going on to Florence, where they had a granddaughter in school. Another was headed to the south of France, where he had been as a paratrooper in World War II. We had plans to go to Paris. But when it came my turn – mind you, after an adequate supply of fine French wine – I impetuously announced that I thought I might head for the Northern Italian town of Alba to buy a truffle dog.

While I surprised even myself with this declaration, I had been thinking about truffles for some time. I had grown up with the aroma and flavor of this exotic (and expensive) member of the mushroom family. Make no mistake, we're not talking about chocolates here. For the uninitiated, the truffle is a subterranean delight. It is a relatively uncommon member of the fungus family that grows entirely underground, taking nourishment from the roots of trees – different trees producing different sorts of truffles.

The Italian white truffle, which grows mainly in the Piemonte region, and the French "Perigord" or black truffle are the ones prized by chefs the world over for their distinctive flavors. Since these culinary treasures, which France's Brillat-Savarin, the first of the "food writers," called "the diamonds of the kitchen," grow wild in woodlands, the hunting of truffles is considered a country art in Italy and France. In France, hunters use trained pigs to sniff out the elusive truffle. But pigs have a bad habit of eating

~ 123 ~

the truffles they find. Italians have trained dogs for this function. Until recent times, attempts to cultivate truffles have ranged from impossible to difficult.

I can personally attest to the charm of the truffle. I grew up eating delicious risotto flavored with Italian truffles. My Piemonte-born parents would receive a supply, generally three or four pounds, every year from their families in Italy.

This was in the 1920s when air transport was not yet available. And truffles, like all fungi, are perishable, so they were packaged in containers of raw rice. This enabled them to retain their quality while also permeating the rice with the strong truffle flavor.

Their arrival at our home, then in Berkeley, was always an occasion for a group of relatives and friends, all of them from the Piedmont area, to gather for a risotto feast, with truffles flavoring just about everything..

I knew that Adolph Moto, who had a restaurant in San Francisco, made news in the *San Francisco Chronicle* when he had a truffle-seeking dog sent to him. He was going to search for truffles in Northern California. I remember that the dog's name was Fido. I don't remember the results of his venture.

Somewhere I had read that there was a man in the town of Roddi, near Alba, who trained dogs to search for truffles. He was known as Professor Barot. In the Piemontese dialect, "barot" is the name of the long staff that is used to unearth the soil around truffles.

On our cruise I had decided to drive to Roddi to meet this Professor Barot and inquire about buying a dog that would find truffles for me at home in Santa Rosa. That simple thought was the spark that exploded into an entire truffle adventure.

Alba, near Turin, is the source of Italian truffles. From Cannes, it is about a three-hour car drive through dozens of tunnels in the Alps. We docked in Cannes and spent a few days exploring the beautiful French Riviera. The Stones, Ralph and Lois, agreed to join us in our truffle adventures. We hired a car and driver and off to Alba we went.

When we arrived at our hotel in Alba, we knew we had come

to the right place. The dining room featured truffles in many different ways – with rice, pasta and salad. We enjoyed them all, becoming more enthusiastic about the dog and the prospects at home. Then, off we went on a tour of the neighboring town of Roddi to find Professor Barot.

Roddi is one of those old, old, medieval towns located on a hill at the very top of which rests its church. We toured up the winding, narrow street to the church, on the very peak of the town. By happenstance, the local priest was there. We asked him if he knew Professor Barot and where he was. He smiled knowingly, and said in Italian I could understand that we might try the local cantina in the middle of town.

As it turned out, Professor Barot was easy to find. Just as we walked up to the entrance to the cantina, which might be described as the Italian equivalent of an Irish pub, a very slight individual came out. He was perhaps 50 years old and carelessly dressed. He flashed a warm smile revealing the absence of several teeth. He wore loose-fitting trousers with the zipper on his fly just about halfway to the top. All this indicated to me that this was a man who enjoyed the pleasures of the wine of the region. I asked him if he knew Professor Barot. He replied, "I am Professor Barot."

Later, I would learn that his true name was Battista Monchiero. And, yes, he had truffle dogs. He invited us to his extremely humble dwelling, two rooms with a small yard. He brought out two little mongrel dogs and explained that they were truffle hunters. I asked if they were for sale. He said no, nor did he know of any that were available. Apparently, a good truffle dog is like a highly prized hunting dog. Their ability to find truffles in the hills around made them extremely valuable. Or so he said. So we thanked him for his time and went back to the French Riviera.

From Nice, the four of us traveled at a leisurely pace to Paris. During the trip, Ralph and I started talking, mostly in fun, about starting a search for truffles in California. The two of us would be the organizers. The friends who were on our ocean voyage would be our investors. We spent considerable time discussing a name for this venture, and, after a great deal of bantering, we came up with "Tristo, "a combination of both our names. We decided Tristo sounded better than "Stotri."

By coincidence, we met Robert and Sharon Lynch at the Ritz hotel in Paris. They were part of our S.S. France group. At dinner – and on into the night, I'm afraid – we regaled them with our truffle plans, embellishing the Tristo project with some grandiose exaggerations.

Molalla Products, remember, owned several thousand acres of timberland. Our friend, Harry Merlo, chairman of Louisiana-Pacific lumber company, had many thousand more acres. We were confident he would give us permission to explore the truffle possibilities on his land in Northern California, including Sonoma, Mendocino and Humboldt counties.

As it happened, Robert Lynch was dining with Jack Smith, a well-known columnist for the *Los Angeles Times.* Lynch told him all about Tristo and our big plans. Smith wrote a column about our grand idea, describing how two wealthy Northern California financiers were seeking to establish a truffle industry in the U.S. The response to the *LA Times* column was electric, particularly from food writers and restaurateurs.

At this point, you understand, I had an extremely limited knowledge of what a truffle was. I knew it grew underground and was some sort of a mushroom. That was it. I decided that the best response to questions was another question, so when the columnists, the chefs and the culinary experts called, I would simply say: "Why not? We have the same Mediterranean climate. Many species of mushrooms grow in our area. Why not truffles?"

After several calls, I began to fear I was in over my head with the prospect of being embarrassed. I called the food and farm division at the University of California at Davis and asked the department operator if anyone in that department knew anything about truffles. She transferred me to one of the associate professors. He said they knew nothing about truffles, but he knew of a professor in the forestry department at Oregon State University in Corvallis who did.

I had lucked out again. The name the professor gave me – that

~ 126 ~

of Dr. James Trappe – turned what could have been a joke that got out of hand into a true scientific study. Dr. Trappe took me seriously. He specialized in mycorrhizal life and was very knowledgeable about truffles. From the first call I made to Jim until this day, we have been very good friends. He explained the overall complexity of fungi. My education began. Jim had written several articles on mycorrhizae, where they exist in the Northwest and in Australia, which has a substantial truffle cultivation program.

Now that we felt legitimate, we had no worries as word of our truffle-hunting plans spread. Inquiries from newspapers throughout the country came in, including the Washington Post, Chicago Tribune and New York Times. In a Sunday feature, the New York Times published an article about these two California financiers who were going to discover truffles in the West. The article was actually quite complete, including how we were going to import dogs for the search. About mid-afternoon of that day, I received a phone call from a man with a heavy accent. This introduction went something like this:

"Meester Trione, my name is Paul Urbani. I am the president of Urbani Truffle Company of America, located in New York. I have just read your article in the New York Times, and I think you and Mr. Stone are a couple of phonies." The inflection in his voice was amicable, and I responded in kind.

"Mr. Urbani, you may be right, " I said.

He continued, "However, if you happen to find any truffles, we would be pleased to be your distributor throughout the United States." This was the second time in the truffle adventure that a phone call initiated a close friendship. That one lasted some 15 years – until Mr. Urbani passed away.

For the next three or four years, Ralph's and my enthusiasm for the truffle hunt endured, although not much happened beyond conversations with people who knew much more than we did. In 1975, Paul Urbani arranged for us to visit his family in Italy. They lived in Umbria, the only province in Italy that does not touch a sea. The four of us conspirators, Lois, Madelyne, Ralph and I were off to Italy again.

We had a good time with Paul's cousin Paolo and his family. The Urbanis' interest as international truffle brokers was backed by their ownership of the local bank and several apartment units. The smell of truffles permeated the "work car" that Paolo drove us around in on a tour of the area.

We discussed the possibility of purchasing two truffle dogs. Yes, Paolo would help us find them. Soon after we returned, through an intermediary, we learned that Paolo had located two truffle dogs. His family would send them via Pan American Airlines. The price was $500 each.

Now, our enthusiasm was in full force. We arranged to hold the first-ever California Truffle Congress. Jim Trappe would come from Oregon with some of his friends and associates. We got permission from the City of Santa Rosa to hold our symposium in the City Council chambers. *The Press Democrat* cooperated by announcing the First Annual Truffle Week.

Then we had a shocker. Paul Urbani called and said, "Paolo decided he didn't want to send the dogs." Whether it was worry about competition that prompted his change of heart, we never knew.

I explained – with some agitation, I confess – that our Truffle Congress was just two weeks away and how much we had counted on the dogs. Paul called back and said, under the circumstances, Paolo had agreed to send them. They would be on Pan Am the next day. Unfortunately, Pan Am in Italy went on strike, so the two dogs lay in their cage for over two days before the flight was rescheduled. They arrived in Oakland the day of the Truffle Congress.

By sheer coincidence, my Palm Springs polo friend Carlton Beal had flown up from Midland, Texas, in his private jet. Because of weather conditions, he had to land his Sabreliner jet in Oakland and was preparing to drive to Santa Rosa when his pilots informed him the weather had cleared enough for the flight to the Sonoma County Airport.

Carlton loaded the dogs on board and they arrived just in time for the Congress opening – in their private jet! My son Victor and

~ 128 ~

his friend Randy Destruel escorted the dogs from the airport to City Hall.

My first thought upon seeing them was that they certainly didn't look "special." Rondanella and Urbetta were two small mongrels, weighing no more than 25 pounds each. But they were nothing if not patient. They attended the entire meeting.

The Truffle Congress was an all-day event, with talks by Jim Trappe and other mycologists. That night, at the Los Robles Lodge, Ralph and I hosted a dinner for more than 100 people. Restaurateur Claus Neumann had seasoned the pasta course with truffles we had ordered from Italy.

The following day the Truffle Congress attendees met at the performing arts facility known then as the Luther Burbank Center for the Arts (now Wells Fargo Center) for morning sessions. The afternoon was spent in oak woodlands north of Healdsburg, searching for that special species of fungi. The Oregon delegates were especially adept and several different species were found. The dogs were there, but declined to participate in anything more than interested sniffs of their new country.

Meanwhile, Paul Urbani was keeping his family in Italy informed about our every action. They may well have been, as I have suggested, concerned about competition, because they sent their representatives from Toronto to pay us visit and report on our activities.

They arrived in a limousine on a Sunday evening at Los Robles Lodge, where we had arranged to meet them. Two husky fellows in their 40s, Paolo and Hugo DiMentitto, had come to watch us hunt truffles with Rondanella and Urbetta.

Next morning Paolo, Hugo, the dogs and I, along with other interested parties, ventured into the hilly, wooded forests of what is now the Wild Oak subdivision. When they were released, the dogs tentatively sniffed the air and took off running. This was not supposed to happen.

Hugo asked, "Do you have wild animals here?" I acknowledged that there were, indeed, deer, rabbits, squirrels and skunks. "No wonder," Hugo said, "they are more interested in hunting animals than seeking the availability of truffles." Eventually, the dogs returned but showed no signs of interest in truffle sites. A tour of the area with them to see if this might be "truffle country" proved negative and the two men returned to Toronto. I suspect they advised the Urbanis that concern over competition was unnecessary.

We kept Rondanella and Urbetta in our horse barn. Soon it became apparent that Urbetta had had an affair with some Italian dog before leaving Italy, for she was now pregnant. We gave Rondanella to Lois Stone, and Urbetta was given to a friend who kept her as a pet and dispersed the litter to friends.

There was another Truffle Congress held 10 years later, also in Santa Rosa. Since that time, much has occurred in the evolution of what can be called a truffle industry. Credit is due Dr. Jim Trappe and his associates. Some of his subsequent research was funded by a grant from Tristo. He has co-authored several significant books, most recently, "Trees, Truffles, and Beasts: How Forests Function."

In Italy and France, truffle societies have existed for decades. Since our last Santa Rosa Truffle Congress, several truffle societies have become very active in this country, including the North American Truffling Society in Corvallis, Oregon.

Eugene, Oregon, hosts the annual three-day Oregon Truffle Festival, which includes a Truffle Growers' Forum, a gourmet dinner, and even truffle dog training. Throughout the Northwest and parts of Texas and Kentucky there are truffle farms developed and developing. One of the most successful varieties of truffle in the U.S. is the Tuber gibbosum, since renamed Tuber Oregon or, more commonly, Oregon White Truffle. It is produced and marketed by several "trufflers." Truffle production has also become very active in Australia, where Jim Trappe spends several weeks a year.

It is beyond my imagination to have thought that a seemingly silly notion aboard the S.S. France in the early 1970s would spark this unique phenomenon I have described. All I ever wanted was to go to Italy to buy a "truffle dog."

One humorous incident evolved from our many newspaper interviews. We needed a "truffle dog" to pose for a photo with Ralph and me. We didn't have a bona fide truffle dog at the time, so we used a mongrel that had wandered into the Wild Oak Stables the week before. We had been trying, unsuccessfully, to give him away. A couple of days after the article and photo were published, a car drove up in the middle of the night and stole the dog! ❖❖❖

CHAPTER XVI ~ WILDLIFE

I have always considered myself a sport hunter and a fisherman, although my lifelong interest in these classic outdoor adventures necessarily took a backseat to my business activity in the early years.

I have hunted and fished my whole life, since my school years in Fortuna where there was a bounty of wildlife in the miles of mountains and forests and in the Eel River virtually at my doorstep.

I want to make it very clear here that I was always a sportsman hunter. That is a term that is important to understand, because society has increasingly rushed to identify anyone participating in the killing of wild animals as inhumane. This is not the case. Taking a wild animal for food is, to a true sportsman, an act that aids the preservation of that creature's species as well as the habitat of all wildlife. With others like myself, I have participated in many organizations that exist to insure wildlife preservation. Two good examples that come immediately to my mind are the California Waterfowl Association and Ducks Unlimited. These and other organizations, dedicated to ecological maintenance of wildlife habitat, are desperately needed as the rapidly increasing human population crowds into the areas that were once wilderness habitat, particularly in the West.

In California's early years, there were no regulations to protect deer or waterfowl or the fish and crab and abalone in the streams and the ocean. In the Gold Rush years, market hunters killed herds of elk and deer and thousands of waterfowl to provide food for "boom town" San Francisco – and later for restaurants in the crowded Bay Area cities. In the rural areas, venison was a primary source of meat. When the California Department of Fish and Game (now Fish and Wildlife) came into existence, preservation gained legal status. State financing provided money to purchase carefully maintained wildlife refuges for migrating waterfowl and protected habitat for animals. Under these conditions, hunters are able to enjoy these sports with clear consciences, with their contributions through license fees and outright donations funding these protective measures.

My first opportunity to enjoy hunting was after our family moved to Santa Rosa. I had become friends with several businessmen who were hunters and belonged to the Folded Hills Hunting Club in Mendocino County (which, some 40 years later, would be the site of my life-threatening riding accident). I was invited to be a member in 1947 and eventually became part owner. The club owned 1,400 acres of hillside land northwest of Cloverdale, surrounded by other large ranches. Deer season in those early years was more than two months long, beginning near the end of July and lasting until the end of September. In other areas, in the northwestern part of the state and the Sierras, deer season is later.

When I joined, Ed Healey, John Galeazzi, Babe Wood and Ralph Brown owned the ranch. Ed Healey's father, Gene Healey, affectionately known as The Colonel, had started the Folded Hills club in the early 1930s. Folded Hills was far from unique. There were dozens of such hunting clubs throughout Northern California. They all followed pretty much the same pattern. Hunting season was also party time. Members would arrive the Friday before opening day of the season. This was an occasion for a reunion celebration, sometimes lasting well into the night. Everyone was awakened at 4 a.m. for a hearty breakfast, in spite of a large, late dinner the night before, following an extended cocktail hour.

Folded Hills had 10 members, each assigned a designated chore. Some worked in the kitchen, others in the skinning shed where the bucks were cleaned and dressed and others on the trails, clearing off debris from the previous spring and winter storms. My first job was culinary, clearing tables and doing dishes. As years went by, I worked my way up to become one of the chefs de cuisine. I drew on my mother's familiar recipes and the members found them very palatable. I would have frequent requests for risotto and veal parmigiano.

There are plenty of amusing anecdotes that could be told of the

~ 133 ~

Folded Hills adventures. I think I'll stick to a safe one. Every year, from the time the club began, someone would order condiments for the season – mustard, pepper, ketchup, hot sauce, things like that. They were always placed in the center of the dining table and left there for the season.

Every year there was a new order, but no one ever moved or removed the old jars and bottles. When I first joined, several years after the club began, there was barely enough room on the table for plates and glasses. Finally, after a long list of wisecracks and snide suggestions, we had a purge and threw away everything and started all over. It was a classic example of a male-only establishment.

After two years, Ralph Brown, one of the four owners, wanted to sell his interest in the club for health reasons. I bought it from him for $4,000.

The club gave me an opportunity to spend time with my sons. I remember the first time Victor went with me. He was eight years old. The first day, on the drive up, I warned him that there would be a lot of what I termed "boy talk" language – and topics – of the sort he was not used to hearing. He was very eager to come along and readily agreed with my new rule that this would be club talk only and was never, ever to be heard at home.

During the off-season, I would bring Madelyne and the two boys there for an overnight or weekend. We always enjoyed ourselves.

I guess I might be considered a Folded Hills survivor – not only because of the 1990 accident, but because of the passage of time. John Galeazzi was the first of the owners to die, then Ed Healy. The last was Babe Wood, who was 102. Our family, meanwhile, had acquired the Flatridge Ranch, 8,000 acres on the Kelly Road west of Cloverdale, and much of our hunting interests were focused there. In time, we agreed to sell our interests to Gary Galeazzi.

He now uses it as a family club.

~ ~ ~ ~ ~

Ducks are quite a different hunting experience. In late October, the duck season opens in Northern California and hunters from all over the state crowd into Butte and Sutter counties in the Sacramento Valley. Many hunting clubs exist there, in the region known to hunters and wildfowl experts as the Butte Sink. This area is on the Pacific Flyway, the course taken by ducks and geese traveling their established migration patterns.

The migration generally commences in October, although it varies according to climate conditions. Flight after flight of ducks, geese and some swans make their way south, traveling as far as Mexico. Northern California is a midpoint resting area. It has been made more attractive to the birds by the many rice fields in the general area. There are a number of state and federal refuges to provide safe habitat and protection from the hunting clubs throughout the area. Shooting times and limits are carefully observed at the clubs, with game wardens to watch for violations. Penalties can be stiff. Duck clubs generally allow shooting only on Wednesdays, Saturdays and Sundays. And wildlife soon learn where the safe resting areas are. So it is truly a sport and by no means a certain duck dinner.

My own introduction to duck hunting came in the 1950s when several older, more experienced hunters from our Santa Rosa area invited me to join them on a Saturday morning shoot. We stayed at a hotel in Willows. During the hunting season, it served as acceptable accommodations for hunters who did not have a clubhouse.

Duck clubs in the Butte Sink area varied in size from four or five members to as many as 40 or 50. Some had elaborate facilities and employees to tend to the needs. Almost all of these clubs were men only, although some clubs would allow wives to join the party on an occasional weekend.

Hunters often rented space in one of the several duck centers. They would park a trailer or build a small clubhouse. Lambertville, five miles east of Willows, was one of these areas. In Lambertville, there were dozens of trailers, Quonset huts and shacks. They were placed at random, not unlike a poorly organized mobile home park.

After two years of going to Willows, it bothered me that I would leave Madelyne and the boys at home. With the cooperation of a builder friend of mine, Walter Pauley, we built a 1,200-square-foot, two-bedroom, very modest cabin. We put it on a 20 x 30-foot lot in Lambertville. We named it the Laughing Mallard Club. Madelyne and Victor and Mark, who were then 12 and 10 years old, could come hunting with me. I would take the boys with me to a duck blind, where they could watch and learn until they were old enough for their own small 20-gauge shotguns.

We hunted out of our Laughing Mallard cabin for three years. And there is one instance from that time none of us will ever forget.

One Saturday morning I placed Mark in a blind close to the road, while Victor and I were in another, about 200 yards away. A flight of snow geese flew over Mark's blind at a height not more than 20 feet. Mark fired one shot. And five geese fell.

Madelyne always remained at the clubhouse. It was pure delight to come back from a damp and chilly morning shoot and find that she had prepared a robust breakfast. We generally returned to Santa Rosa on Sunday afternoon. But there was one memorable weekend, when there was an extremely heavy rainstorm, that we took a "slight" detour. We left the cabin about noon and, as we started home, I could see, in the distance, vast flights of birds. Since it was early, I decided it would be a good time to take the family through the refuge to get a closer look.

We headed for the Sacramento National Wildlife Refuge, contiguous to Lambertville, that was the resting place for thousands of birds and is really something to see. The entrance, where the office and administrative buildings are, is off the main highway. Then the road goes due east for three or four miles. We had traveled more than a mile, looking at the waterfowl, observing flights, when I decided to turn back and head for home.

Since the road was quite narrow, I took a road to the right, assuming it would go to another parallel road taking us back to the main entrance.

I went about 500 yards before the road got very narrow and turned to mud. The wheels on my Cadillac sank, and we were hopelessly stuck. Leaving Madelyne and the boys in the car, I ran the whole distance to the headquarters hoping to find some help. As I came to an employee's cottage, a young man came out to smoke a cigarette. I explained my predicament. We hopped in his Jeep with a tow rope and drove out to my car. While connecting the rope to what he could find of the car above the mud, he himself became muddy – and not very pleased about it. Finally, he started the Jeep to pull the car out of the mud. The Jeep couldn't get traction, slipped to the side and was stuck.

After several tries, he stopped speaking and left. After about half an hour, he came up the refuge road with a road grader. He attached the grader to the Jeep, then to my car. The grader got stuck. So, there it was. The car, the Jeep and the grader thoroughly mired in deep mud. The young man was nothing if not tenacious. He went back to the main area again and returned with a very serious tractor made for heavy-duty roadwork. There were iron cleats on the wheels that left deep holes on the road. About this time, the main warden, who had been watching all this activity from his own house, appeared on the scene. He was furious.

If anyone was ever read a riot act, it was I. All I could do was remain quiet and humbly say, "Yes, sir," over and over again. Inside, I was saying a little prayer, asking God to get me out of this mess, which I had created. Finally, one after the other, the vehicles were removed. After stern admonishments and strict orders not to return, ever, we left. We made it home by 10 p.m., about six hours past the customary time to end our duck hunting weekends.

Although we enjoyed Lambertville, I was never comfortable with the closeness of the rented hunting blinds to each other. I learned from a local real estate broker, who specialized in selling and renting clubs in the Lambertville area, that there was a 250-acre club for sale to the east, between Colusa and Gridley.

One Sunday, about noon, the family and I followed him to the Tule Goose Club, some three miles south of the main Colusa-Gridley highway.

The caretaker, who lived in a very basic cabin, was Fred Lynch. His wife, Liz, was the cook. Fred took us out to the ponds and blinds, which were only 400 or 500 yards away. The ponds were loaded with ducks of all species, mostly Pintail and Mallard. It was absolutely ideal. If there was ever something I wanted, the Tule Goose Club was it.

The broker advised me that the club's owners wanted to sell because they were advancing in age. Their spokesman was Milton Nauheim, the West Coast vice president of National Distilleries. As a tradition, at every meeting he handed the visitor a bottle of one of the brands of whiskey his company offered. I considered it a nice, friendly gesture. In final negotiations, we agreed on a price of $160,000 in four annual payments of $40,000 each. The Tule Goose Club, with 220 acres, became ours.

Some of the duck clubs in the Butte Sink area go back as far as the 1880s. Records showed that the Tule Goose was started in 1906. Nauheim's group acquired it in the 1930s for $4,000. Access then was by boat down the canal from the Colusa–Gridley highway. Water for the ponds was pumped from the canal to the five ponds.

Sometime in the 1940s, natural gas had been discovered in the area. Two gas wells were on the Tule Goose property. To have proper access to the wells, the gas company built a road along the canal from the highway to the property. At the insistence of Nauheim, it was graveled and paved to a very good condition. He further insisted upon, and received, free fuel for heating the cabin. Electricity was also provided. In addition, Nauheim received negotiated revenue for the gas. He retained these rights, but upon acquiring the club we were given free fuel for the clubhouse.

Our weekends with family and friends at Tule Goose are very happy memories. Because wives were invited, we called them "Powder Puff" weekends. Some of our neighbors weren't pleased at this because, up until we bought the club, hunting there had been exclusively male.

Shooting was particularly good. The most prevalent species around our club was the Pintail. On occasion we saw Mallard, Gadwall or Wood Duck. Invariably, we would get a Spoonbill, also called a Spoonie, or as the family named it, a Laughing Mallard. A very successful shoot was a limit of seven Pintail ducks. If a hunter shot a Spoonbill, he was given a card identifying him as Mr. Soup-lips. At the suggestion of our friend and frequent guest Wayne Ancel, we ceremoniously had the shooter kiss a mounted Spoonbill we had hung on the wall for that purpose. These "rituals" added to the fun.

The cabin at Tule Goose was probably built in the '20s. It had three small bedrooms, one-and-a-half baths. It was located down below the canal road, so that during rains the area below the ground floor flooded. One Wednesday, I invited my architect friend, Germano Milono, to the club.

When he observed the location and quality of the club, he said, "You're living in a shack in a mud-hole." He sketched out a two-story, six-bedroom, house with a large dining room and quarters for the manager. To me, the thought of my investing the amount of money needed to build the lodge was out of the question. But, as years went by, Madelyne, Victor and Mark insisted. So we built from the plans that Milono had prepared. The building project took three years.

Before we began the new building, the caretaker, Fred Lynch, announced that he felt he was not pleasing us and had decided to retire. He recommended Gene Shockley and his wife, Wanda, to live on the property. Gene was a six-foot plus, 300-pound giant of a man known as "Fats" to his friends. The employment of the Shockleys proved to be a very satisfactory arrangement. They lived there year-round and maintained the property in top condition. They had living quarters to themselves all but the three months of duck season and the occasional weekend when we visited.

One early morning, Gene awakened to the smell of smoke. The building was on fire. He and Wanda had just enough time to put on clothes. They escaped at the last second with nothing of their belongings. With no phone service at the club (and, of course, no cell phones yet) the Shockleys drove to the nearest occupied duck club, three miles away, to call the fire department. By the time the fire trucks arrived, the house was in a full blaze that could be seen for miles.

~ 139 ~

What remained were the concrete foundations, and nothing more. We immediately redrew the plans. We expanded and extended some rooms. Today it remains a very comfortable lodge, enjoyed by all the family during the season. In the interim, Gene Shockley has died and Wanda has retired. Our caretakers now are R.C. and Helen Cox, who do an excellent job. As the years went by, ownership in duck clubs increased and the values grew accordingly. The story of what happened to the Tule Goose is a splendid example of what you might call "The Luck of the Triones."

As I have already stated, the purchase price of the club was $160,000. There was, of course, a substantial cost to operate a club – not only caretakers' wages but the expense of providing water to the ponds, plus electricity and equipment to service them. Before we bought the club, the Department of Fish and Game had created the Gray Lodge Refuge. It ultimately evolved into several thousand acres of resting ponds and public shooting areas. The many ponds in this refuge required a free flow of clear water (as distinguished from stagnant water) which made drainage outlets essential. Previous owner Nauheim had granted the state a right-of-way through the Tule Goose property to the main canal in exchange for which the club would have access to free water.

Some years after we acquired the Tule Goose, federal funds became available, through the California Natural Resources Agency, to assure that no land in the wildlife preservation area would be converted to agricultural use. In the case of Tule Goose, the surrounding area was predominantly rice fields. The government was moving to prevent any further of cultivation of waterfowl habitat. In exchange for signing an easement keeping the land forever wild, we received $1,000 an acre or $220,000. It had been a duck club for the better part of a century and we had no intention of becoming rice farmers. But the Feds paid us anyway.

Meanwhile, the gas wells were no longer producing. The five natural gas wells in the fields were exhausted, and the production ceased. However, a Houston, Texas, company brought offers to the owners of land with existing wells. They wanted to lease the exhausted area for the storage of gas that would be piped down from Canada for distribution throughout Northern California. As it turned out, the storage of gas or oil is not a matter of mineral rights such as those that Nauheim and his partners had retained. Storage areas are an asset of the landowner. Our share of the former gas fields was 17 percent. Owners of the neighboring Wild Goose Club owned over 80 percent of the fields. The Wild Goose Club led the negotiations. And one of their members proved to be very good at it. The annual leasing rent was $1 million dollars a year with a 4 percent annual increase. For us this reflects an annual return of $170,000 on our investment. Needless to say, this has added to our continued enjoyment of our duck club. It has been suggested that Tule Goose is the one that laid a golden egg.

~ ~ ~ ~ ~

Our Sonoma County ranch – which came to us as a result of our investment in Molalla timber – has become another treasured spot for the family. The 1,150 acres of land that we bought from Lucile Kelly, off the private Kelly Road between Cloverdale and the ocean, has grown to some 9,000 acres or more in that area with the acquisition of the Flatridge Ranch from the Norton family. Now owned by Mark and Victor, Flatridge is about a two-hour drive from home – eight miles from the turn-off from the Kelly Road, 17 miles in from Cloverdale, about halfway to Annapolis.

This ranch, which I still call The Kelly, is a haven of wildlife and very pleasant rural living. The nearest neighbors are nine miles away. Now, thanks to cellular phones, it's not as remote as it once was. But it can be as remote as you want it to be. Mostly covered with Douglas fir, some pine and some redwoods, it has two year-round streams, 84 miles of passable Jeep roads and one 10-acre lake.

The picnic area is flat and lightly wooded with an open kitchen, including all the necessary appliances, a large open pit fireplace and six comfortable one-room cottages. They are named Hassler, for the famous Rome hotel, the Paris Ritz, the Palace, the Mark Hopkins, the St. Francis and the Clift. Who could ask for better accommodations? And no traffic noise.

In addition, Mark has built his lodge: a well-constructed four-bedroom lodge contiguous to the river, made of prime redwood, logged and sawed on the ranch by our managers, Jerry and Katie Lewers. Since Jerry's death his son David Lewers and his wife, Bunny, run the entire ranch. Inside the well-furnished lodge rooms are many of Mark's mounted trophies from hunts through the years: deer, elk, moose, wolves and coyotes. ❖❖❖

CHAPTER XVII ~ CHECKING MY LIST

In the back pages of this long look at my long life, there is a list of recognitions that some would say result from good deeds done. I would not take that kind of credit. I would call them privileges and opportunities.

I have been privileged, because of good fortune in very good times, to have opportunities to share with charities I have been involved in through the years, ranging from higher education to wildlife.

I could not possibly go into detail about all the things on that list – certainly not without sounding like I was just tooting my own horn. But there are several of these charitable adventures that seem to me to be interesting enough to share.

~ ~ ~ ~ ~

The first one – at least in chronological order – is the conversion of a troubled church to a highly successful performing arts center. In 1981, a religious congregation with a building complex just north of Santa Rosa known as the Christian Life Center got into a series of difficult situations that resulted in bankruptcy. The buildings included an auditorium and classrooms and seemed ready-made for conversion. We looked at it, initially, as a possible home for Empire College.

Meanwhile, Santa Rosa, coming from a decade of the largest population increase in its history, was without a proper venue for its excellent symphony orchestra or for visiting performers. Several influential members of the Santa Rosa Rotary Club, interested in finding an appropriate space, had created a non-profit entity called the Luther Burbank Memorial Foundation. When the Christian Life Center became available, it seemed well-suited for their purposes. The Burbank Foundation decided that it would bid to buy the complex when it came up for auction in the courts. All it lacked was the money.

Let me be clear that I wasn't the idea man here. Others had

~ 143 ~

seen the potential in the building before I became involved. I heard what my golfing friend Rod McNeill, who was one of the foundation members, had to say and I made some calls to see if there was support from others. We figured that if we could get a dozen couples to invest, we could raise several million dollars, enough for a reasonable bid. This was early August. The auction date was set for September. We had three weeks to come up with the money.

Our rationalization was the value of the buildings. We knew that the money we put up would be only a fraction of what the complex was worth. The value was about $20 million; with the amount of our contributions about $5 million. If we donated a $20 million facility to the foundation, the tax deductibility factor for persons with higher incomes meant that our $5 million in contributions cost us practically nothing.

All I did was make the early move. It took a lot of friends to make the deal. Evert Person and his wife Ruth, owners of *The Press Democrat*, agreed to help, as did Lois and Ralph Stone, Nell and Hugh Codding and Marion and Ed Gauer. Ed was the former owner of Roos/Atkins department stores who had retired to Alexander Valley. This was the extent of my support group when I walked into Judge Conley Brown's federal courtroom on September 1. There were 200 people there to watch – some to participate. There were members of the church who hoped to buy it back, as well as a Sebastopol man who owned a chain of convalescent hospitals who was prepared to bid.

We made a cash offer of $4.5 million, payable in 30 days. Rod McNeill liked to tell people afterward that I turned to him and said, "You S.O.B., look what you've got me into." It's true that it looked pretty shaky. We had exactly half of the dozen couples we needed to complete the deal. We had just 30 days to find six more. I anchored the bid with a cashier's check, and we formed a corporation – CLC Development Company – which promptly leased the complex to the Luther Burbank Memorial Foundation for a dollar a month, plus 20 percent of the revenue.

And then we went out and found the rest of the backers. We

actually had to find seven more, as the Gauers had dropped out. The support, as it turned out, was there. The group which the newspaper took to calling "Henry's Angels" expanded to include Rosemary and Benny Friedman (Friedman Brothers Hardware), Gloria and Chester Galeazzi (Eagle Distributing), Dolores and John Headley (Yardbirds), Catherine and Gerald Ayers (Chevron distributorship), Betty and Tom Freeman (Toyota dealership), Olive and Bob Kerr (Standard Structures), and Lori and Bill Manly (Honda dealership).

The Santa Rosa Symphony immediately became the first permanent tenant. Comedian Steve Allen was the first headliner. He packed the auditorium. In the end, we passed title for the complex to the Luther Burbank Foundation, the owner of the Luther Burbank Center for the Arts. It is now known as the Wells Fargo Center – a gesture to the corporation that provided needed funding more than two decades later.

Star of the Valley

It was that same year – 1981 – that the Diocese of Santa Rosa began to explore the possibility of a new Catholic parish to serve the population in the Kenwood area, including Oakmont and Wild Oak. The bishop of the Santa Rosa Diocese, Mark Hurley, assigned this task to Monsignor Gerard Fahey, who was then completing his decade as pastor of St. Eugene's Cathedral in Santa Rosa.

The first Masses in the parish were held in a hall at Santa Rosa Junior College's police academy at Los Guilucos and at a Kenwood restaurant then known as Ray's Rancho, later the Kenwood Restaurant. And Father Fahey began his search for property to build a church. The initial plan was to look for a site in Kenwood but as the parish rolls expanded it became apparent that the center of population growth was in and around Oakmont. Land there was not only expensive but not readily available in the acreage necessary. As it happened, we owned land on a corner, two acres across from the polo fields. It was very brushy, with several big, old oak trees. It was a perfect setting. We donated it to the diocese. My

~ 145 ~

son Victor's first house became the parish residence.

This decision would undoubtedly have come as a surprise to my parents. Both came from business-oriented families in Italy that had lost contact with the Roman Catholic Church in the 1800s, at the time of the "Resorgimento" when Giuseppe Garibaldi's unification of the country was opposed by the Papacy. Both Trione and Bertalino ancestors supported Garibaldi and not the Church.

Neither my father nor my mother were churchgoers. And, consequently, neither was I in my early years, although I had been baptized, taken catechism and First Communion and been confirmed, almost routinely, as a Catholic.

My secular attitudes continued through my college years and the military. But Madelyne and I were married by a Catholic priest and when we settled in Santa Rosa and became part of the community, it seemed important that our boys be raised in that faith.

Gradually, I came to appreciate the basic teachings of Catholicism and to look forward to that comfortable hour of meditation each week as an observance of all the beauty we see in life and of gratitude for what has been given me. While I consider myself a practicing Catholic and am pleased and proud of my family of regular churchgoers, I thoroughly respect the convictions of all people, whatever their denominations may be. All are based on faith and one's convictions are one's own.

We were pleased and proud to be able to have a part in the "birth" of the new parish church in the Diocese of Santa Rosa. Santa Rosa architect Bill Knight designed the new church, which we asked to be similar to the one we attend in Palm Desert, a design that takes advantage of the surrounding views. We had hoped the church could be situated on the property so there would be a view of Hood Mountain. But Bishop Hurley was afraid the parishioners would have the sun in their eyes and told the architect to turn it around.

We also asked that the church be named St. Catherine's, in honor of my mother. Bishop Hurley vetoed that as well, because, he said, there was another St. Catherine's in the diocese. He named the church Star of the Valley. Later, the chapel at Santa Rosa Memorial Hospital was called St. Catherine's, just as the chapel at the Catholic Cemetery is named for my late wife, Madelyne.

Star of the Valley Catholic Church was dedicated August 15, 1984, with services conducted by Bishop Hurley and Monsignor Fahey, who had watched over the construction so carefully that his parishioners came to refer to him as the "sidewalk superintendent."

The Lone Sailor

In 1970, a quarter of a century after my active duty in World War II came to an end, I became a board member of the U.S. Navy Memorial Foundation in Washington, D.C. This foundation is headquartered on Pennsylvania Avenue, where an impressive memorial and the adjacent Naval Heritage Center honor all men and women of the United States Sea Services, past and present. The centerpiece of the memorial is a 100-foot diameter granite map of the world with the bronze statue of a sailor prominently displayed, surrounded by 26 large bronze panels commemorating events in Naval history. The statue, a bit larger than life, is by sculptor Stanley Bleifeld.

I had always admired the statue. When I joined the board, I argued constantly (and sometimes contentiously) that while San Francisco was one of the great natural seaports of the world – a major embarkation point for 1.5 million men and women during WWII, home to two naval air stations and two shipyards – there was no site to recognize, much less honor, the men and women who had sailed from here to do their duty for America.

I argued that it was time to repair this oversight and that a similar statue should be established on the West Coast – preferably in San Francisco. The board listened patiently and finally said in effect: "If you think you can do it, we will support you. But you will have to secure your own site, your own funds and your own political permissions." I decided to accept the challenge. As a starting point, I sent a letter to a few of my friends I felt would be supportive of the idea. The letter dated August 18, 1997, read:

"Gentlemen:

This will confirm our luncheon date at the Pacific-Union Club on Wednesday, September 3, at 12 noon.

This is not a fund-raising occasion, so don't get nervous. It's to explore the feasibility of developing a memorial in the environs of the city of San Francisco, dedicated to veterans and members of the Sea Services (Coast Guard, Marines, Merchant Marines and Navy).

As a member of the board of directors of the Navy Memorial Foundation, Admiral Henry McKInney, President and CEO, has asked me to chair this program. I, therefore, am most appreciative of your interest and participation.

Eat well and sleep warm."
"Henry"

I was pleased to host six men, all veterans, who would be on board for the duration of the project. They were: Jackson Schultz, Martin McNair, David Nelson, Paul "Red" Fay, Edward Hochuli and Wilber Lucas. That meeting was the first of many that would follow in the next five years, until the project was complete.

Our first stumbling block was the search for a site in San Francisco. It was unsuccessful for a number of reasons, but primarily because of the hostile attitude of the city fathers toward anything military. An attempt to secure a site at the south end of the Golden Gate Bridge was also unsuccessful, because it had been promised for another project. On the day we got that bad news we were driving home across the bridge to Santa Rosa when my friend, David Nelson, a former newspaperman and lobbyist, suggested we turn off the bridge at Vista Point.

We did, and drove on to a scruffy dirt area with a weather-beaten kiosk in the middle and a glorious view of the bridge, the city and the entire East Bay. I was greatly impressed and asked if the land was available. Nelson had no idea who the land belonged to, but he promised to start a search.

That year-long search took us on a parade of ownerships, including the United States Army, the State of California and the U.S. Department of the Interior. All had held title to the Vista Point site at one time or another.

Happily, it turned out that its immediate jurisdiction was under the Superintendent of the Golden Gate National Recreation Area.

We established a rapport with the staff of this federal office and, after a few tense meetings of the commission in charge, we received a heart-warming letter from the Secretary of the Interior that not only approved the project but wished us well and asked that he be invited to the dedication.

Now all systems were go. We hired Fred Warnecke, a young and very talented landscape architect, to design the memorial. He made regular reports to our committee and came up with a plan that used the Bleifeld sailor and a recasting of the Sea Services plaques, with Sacramento Valley artist and sculptor Keith Christie commissioned to design the Navy plaque, which includes the Golden Gate Bridge in the background. I had appointed Jackson Schultz, a Navy captain retired from the Supply Corps, to be my co-chairman. He became our chief fundraiser and over the next two years his committee raised $3 million for the project – all private donations, large and small.

The Warnecke plan was executed by Ridgeview Builders of Santa Rosa. Their on-site supervisor, Richard Brown, made the project his own. Brown tells the very touching story of how ex-servicemen would come to the construction site and surreptitiously drop their dog tags into the hollow cement block that forms the core of the monument. Hearing that meant a great deal to me.

We were determined from the beginning that this would be a first-class job. So we sent both Warnecke and the granite contractor, Robert Cunningham, to Europe to select the stone to celebrate the pride we felt in the monument we were creating. The stones selected came from four continents – Verde Oliva and

Verde Maritaka from Brazil; Ruby Red from India; Belfast Black from South Africa; Absolute Black from Zimbabwe; and Luna Pearl from Italy. All of the rough stones were fabricated in Italy to exact sizes. Completed, the plaza contains more than 1,100 individual granite pieces cut into 300 different shapes and sizes. The largest stone weighed more than 1,200 pounds and the smallest only a few ounces.

Then came the day that the Lone Sailor, with his duffel bag at his side, arrived from the sculptor. A huge crane swung him onto the pedestal that had been prepared for his vigil, facing the bridge and looking out to sea. At that moment, we all saw the end of the task and knew that a dedication date was not far away. The project had been great fun for all of us and the new friendships that we made still exist at this writing. I usually have a reunion for all of my colleagues on the project once a year. We are all very proud of our work and are happy to see how well visitors from all over the world have accepted it.

On dedication day, April 14, 2002, Washington sent an appropriate collection of Navy brass, including the Secretary of Veterans Affairs. Everyone spoke glowingly of our labors. The morning was clear and the air was crisp as the Navy Band played Sousa marches. The atmosphere was one of great pride in a job well done. The speeches were patriotic and inspiring. The day ended with a celebratory luncheon at the St. Francis Yacht Club, directly across the bay from the monument.

Since that time it has been estimated that more than two million visitors a year come to see the statue, many to be photographed next to it and some to rub the edge of the sailor's bronze pea-jacket, which modern legend says will bring good luck. As a final formality, we deeded title to the memorial to the California Department of Transportation, which now has the responsibility for operating and maintaining the H. Dana Bowers Memorial Vista Point site. Much credit belongs to Jackson Schultz who took it upon himself to supervise the monument construction and see that it is maintained in good condition. At this writing, this is still his job.

Trust Funds

Finally, I want to explain my most recent charitable adventure – one that has brought me much satisfaction. As I have said before, throughout my business career I have always been concerned about what happened to my father after he sold the Humboldt County bakery in the 1920s, moved to the Bay Area where my mother was more comfortable with family and friends, and invested his hard-earned money in margin accounts. In October of 1929 came Black Friday, when the stock market crashed and his margins were wiped out. He was left with somewhat less than what the family needed and, consequently, had to go back to Fortuna and the bakery.

This had a substantial effect on his life and the life of our family. It was a lesson to me never to put my family in a vulnerable position. I have made a practice of selling prematurely, you might say, sacrificing a portion of what might have been earned, rather than take a risk.

In 1995, when I was 75, Madelyne and I set up the first of three charitable remainder trusts, totaling, at the time of the investment, some $10 million. We named more than a dozen beneficiaries, all of them charities I have been privileged to be involved with through the years.

The trusts were to provide a 7 percent interest income for me and my family until I died, with the principal to be divided among the charities upon my death.

Despite my lifelong care to avoid economic downturns, the national and international financial crises of 2008 cost me roughly half the value of the three trusts. While there has been some recovery, I concluded, at the age of 91, that it would be better to liquidate the trusts and see the beneficiaries enjoy the benefits of these funds.

The trusts were liquidated in 2013. My 7 percent income was eliminated but I had the satisfaction of seeing the cash benefits go to the charitable institutions I had been supportive of through the years. These non-profits had been affected by the financial downturn as well and the funds were well received. The

~ 151 ~

organizations benefitting from the three charitable remainder trusts in 2013:

- Santa Rosa Memorial Hospital Foundation for both the capital campaign and the Norma and Evert Person Heart and Vascular Institute
- Sonoma State University Academic Foundation
- Donald and Maureen Green Music Center
- Community Foundation of Sonoma County
- Historical Museum of Sonoma County
- Catholic Charities and the Catholic Community Foundation of the Diocese of Santa Rosa
- University of California, Berkeley
- Humboldt State University
- Luther Burbank Memorial Foundation
- California State Parks Foundation
- Volunteer Center of Sonoma County
- United States Navy Memorial Foundation
- California Waterfowl Association
- Ducks Unlimited
- Canine Companions for Independence
- Cardinal Newman High School
- Ursuline High School

I have always felt that it is the obligation of fortunate people to share their good fortune with their communities, whether with gifts of money or gifts of their time. Working with non-profit organizations, I came to realize quickly how much they rely on that support and how essential it is that we all accept that responsibility. Also, I have to say that it has given me great personal pleasure to hear from these groups what things have been made possible by the distribution of these trusts.

As many of my friends know, I am fond of quoting the industrialist Armand Hammer who liked to remind people that, "There are no luggage racks on a hearse." ❖❖❖

TWICE BLESSED

More than half of my life was spent with a wonderful woman named Madelyne Victorina Keyes. From the day we were married in 1946 until the day she died in 2002, Madelyne was the other side of me.

For 56 years she was the partner who listened to my bright ideas, wild and otherwise, and made sound suggestions about business plans. Our mindsets were much the same, although I have to admit she was quick to challenge any concept of mine she felt was not in our mutual best interest.

She was the hostess who entertained our many friends as well as the people I invited to our home for business reasons. She was the world's best traveling companion. She was smart and funny and very attractive. Together, and with our sons, we saw the world.

We made several trips to Italy, including visits to the Vatican. We traveled on barges through the canals of France, vacationed in Mexico and made the most of business (and polo) trips to Argentina and Australia. We were invited by United Airlines to fly on the first DC-8 jet trip from San Francisco to New York in 1959 – in those days, a great adventure. In our later years we spent our winters at our comfortable home in Palm Desert.

The longest and most eventful of our travels came in 1964 when the family went on a 30-day safari to Central Africa. Just getting there was part of the adventure, particularly for the boys, who were teenagers at the time. On the way to Nairobi, we went to Rome for a full review of the Vatican. From there, we went to Rabat, Beirut and Jerusalem, where we walked the Stations of the Cross. Next we were off to Cairo, where we rode around the Sphinx on camels. Then we made our way to Dar es Salaam and on to Nairobi.

When Madelyne died in 2002 it was as if a shroud had been cast over my life from which I felt I would never be free. The loneliness of a widower was a burden of which I did not expect to be relieved. But one day, two years after Madelyne's death, I had dinner with Eileen Ryan and some friends. Madelyne and I had often enjoyed the company of Eileen and her husband John, before John's death several years earlier.

It all happened in the best possible way. Neither Eileen nor I was "looking." But it happened that our personalities seemed to click. We were married at Star of the Valley Catholic Church in 2006. I am particularly appreciative of the warm family relationship Eileen has given me with her three sons, Jim, John and Kevin, with their wives, Kellie, Kim and Martha.

My life has changed much for the better since that happy day and we enjoy a most warm and loving companionship.

God has been very good to me. ❖❖❖

PATS ON THE BACK

- University of California Alumni Excellence in Achievement Award
- California State Parks Foundation – Chairman Emeritus – 1969 – 1999
- Sonoma County Trail Blazers – President – 1971-1976
- Santa Rosa Chamber of Commerce Businessman of the Decade Award – 1973
- Sonoma State University Honorary Degree – June 1, 1979
- City of Oakland Salutes Henry Trione – Oakland Raiders – 1980
- The White House – Ronald Reagan (for State Parks Foundation) – 1982
- Boy Scouts Sonoma-Mendocino Area Council Distinguished Citizen – 1982
- Ducks Unlimited Luncheon Sponsor – November 1984
- Sonoma State School of Business & Economics Honor – 1987
- Humboldt State University – Who's Who Award – 1988
- United States Navy Commander in Chief – October 11, 1989
- Doctorate, Humanities – Sonoma State University – 1990
- Personal Home Care of California – Patient of the Year – 1990
- City of Santa Rosa Proclamation Award – 1990
- National Italian American Foundation Award – October 1991
- SIR – Sons in Retirement – 1992
- Award of Merit California State Parks Foundation – 1992
- Cardinal Newman – 1994 Board of Regents
- Mayor of Fortuna Class of 1937 Award – 1996
- Honorary Member Winemaker Pink Onion (Bohemian Club) – 1997
- United Way Pioneer Award – 1997
- Alumni of the Year – University of California, Berkeley – 1997

- Sonoma County Arts Council – Distinguished Citizen Award – 2000
- North Bay Lifetime Entrepreneurship Noble Award – 2000
- Santa Rosa Memorial Hospital – James & Billie Keegan Leadership Series Award – 2000
- Alumni of the Year – Navy Supply Corps, U.S. Navy – 2000
- Republic of Italy Order of Commandatore – June 28, 2001
- Social Advocates for Youth Award – 2002
- San Francisco Chronicle Salute to U.S. Sailors – April 2002
- Sonoma County Trail Blazers "Old Guard" award – June 2002
- United States Navy Memorial Foundation – Lone Sailor Appreciation Award – 2002
- Maritime Heritage Award – November 19, 2002
- City of San Francisco Proclamation – Henry Trione Day – November 19, 2002
- California Human Development Award – 2003
- Navy Supply Corps School Distinguished Alumnus Award – April 11, 2003
- Sonoma State University – Redwood Society Most Distinguished Citizen Award – April 2003
- Navy Supply Corps Foundation – September 25, 2003
- Sonoma County Farm Bureau Hall of Fame – Nov. 15, 2003
- Sons of Italy Humanitarian Award – 2003
- Associazione Piemontesi nel Mondo Grateful Appreciation Award – 2004
- Chair, Lone Sailor United States Navy Memorial – 2004
- Caltrans District 4, Excellence in Transportation Award – 2004
- Santa Rosa Police Officers – Guardian Angel Award – 2005
- Overseer – Hoover Institute/Stanford University – 2006
- Sonoma County DSA K9 – 2007
- Fortuna Union High School 70th Class Anniversary Award – August 2007
- Arts Council of Sonoma County Honoree – Sept. 8, 2007
- California State Parks Foundation – Golden Poppy Award – October 13, 2007

- California State Park Ranger Foundation – Honorary Ranger – 2008
- Sonoma County Fair – The Horse Industry – Outstanding Horseman – 2008
- U.S. Polo Association, Hall of Fame – 2008
- Haas School of Business, UC Berkeley, Hall of Fame – 2013

QUOTATIONS I'VE REMEMBERED
THROUGH THE YEARS

~ "I've been rich and I have been poor and being rich is better."
– Shirley MacLaine

~ "Who says it doesn't pay to worry? Everything I worry about never happens." – Unknown

~ "The good thing about telling the truth is you don't have to remember what you said." – Unknown

~ "I believe in giving my children enough to do something, but not enough to do nothing." – Warren Buffett

~ "Blessed be he who expects nothing for he will not be disappointed." – Ruby Codding Hall, Hugh Codding's mother

~ "Help a friend when he is down and out and he will never forget you. Particularly the next time he is down and out."
– Unknown

~ "Everything in moderation, even moderation." – Unknown

~ Re: Golf and golf clubs, "It's not the arrow, it's the Indian."
– Lee Trevino

~ "The only person that wants to live to 100 years is the person who is 99 years old." – Unknown

~ "One martini, two martini, three martini, floor."
– Personal experience

~ "If you do not know where you are going, any road will take you there." – Unknown